Touchdown from Heaven
In the huddle with Felicia Young

By Felicia Young

To _____

From _____

authorHOUSE®

AuthorHouse™
1663 Liberty Drive
Bloomington, IN 47403
www.authorhouse.com
Phone: 1-800-839-8640

© 2011 Felicia Young. All rights reserved.

No part of this book may be reproduced, stored in a retrieval system, or transmitted by any means without the written permission of the author.

First published by AuthorHouse 5/5/2011

ISBN: 978-1-4567-3557-9 (e)
ISBN: 978-1-4567-3558-6 (hc)
ISBN: 978-1-4567-3559-3 (sc)

Library of Congress Control Number: 2011901623

*All scriptures are written in the King James Version

Printed in the United States of America

Any people depicted in stock imagery provided by Thinkstock are models, and such images are being used for illustrative purposes only. Certain stock imagery © Thinkstock.

This book is printed on acid-free paper.

Because of the dynamic nature of the Internet, any web addresses or links contained in this book may have changed since publication and may no longer be valid. The views expressed in this work are solely those of the author and do not necessarily reflect the views of the publisher, and the publisher hereby disclaims any responsibility for them.

DEDICATION

Our Father who are in Heaven, I give all Reverence unto You for saving my life by giving me Jesus Christ, my Savior and Lord, for pulling me out of that darkness I was in and you place me into your marvelous light. I am safe, save and sanctified with Your Spirit of love, grace, and mercy. You taught me to believe, trust, and have faith in you. That's everything to me.

I say thank you to my grandparents, Smith and Eliza Owens, my parents Bonnie King, and Herman Wynne for praying for me, my children Lakesha, Vintrisa, Vincent Jr. for believing in me and forgiving me, along with my baby brother Herman Jerod, all my neighbors, relatives and friends, for supporting me.

Also my beloved brother Keith who came back and got me in my dream and took me to church letting me know that this was the way.

My changed life is a testimony so I dedicate this book to all who is seeking God to deliver them out of darkness like He did me.

Foreword

Congresswoman Sheila Jackson Lee

This book is a powerful story by a woman of God who has seen reformation in her own life and now is sharing it with the world. Felicia Young's life story is an inspiration to mothers, families, persons who have lost their way and those human beings who have fallen to the lowest point in their lives. Both Felicia and I love sports, and *Touchdown from Heaven* uses sports acronyms to tell her story. This sports format will make this book fun, exciting to read while leaving you eager to finish. I have seen Felicia Young share her generous spirit, capacity for life, and love of family with the broader community. She has inspired her son, renown football player Vince Young, and I know he is also proud of his mother. This book will touch the hearts of people around the world, leave lives changed – certainly smiles will be seen and souls will be saved. Felicia Young has written a book that will give her the title of "Public Servant" for God

Congresswoman Sheila Jackson Lee
Houston, Texas

The former Mayor Wife Mrs. Elsye Lanier

I have had the privilege of knowing Felicia Young for many years and know first-hand her dedication to her ministry. Her debut book, *Touchdown from Heaven*, is a wonderful and fascinating account of her transformation from a single mother struggling with addiction, poverty and violence to the strong, fulfilled woman of faith she is today. Through her Felicia Young Ministries, she is working to empower other women in crisis and helping them change their lives. *Touchdown from Heaven* is a must-read for anyone who wants to know how faith can make a difference.

Dr. Samuel H. Smith, Senior Pastor

This book is another bold example of God's love for His own. I have no doubt Felicia Young's spiritual growth now guides her heart and hand as she shares her life-altering experiences, which will encourage readers to actively pursue a faith-based loving relationship with God and His son, Christ Jesus.

What a blessing in store for those who accept Christ, now the Lord of her life and the means of our salvation. I am grateful to God for allowing our paths to cross. Knowing her family both personally and spiritually as members of the body of Christ at the Horeb Church, while witnessing their growth serves to reinforce the fact that God loves us.

I am sure this book will be a blessing to readers of all ages. *Touchdown from Heaven* evidences the Holy Spirit at work, using Felicia as its vehicle to a renewed faith in God, the true blessing.

Dr. Samuel H. Smith, Senior Pastor
Mount Horeb Missionary Baptist Church
Houston, Texas

Vince Young

"My mother's work and vision has already reached many people in need of spiritual guidance and love. I am proud of the many years and countless lives that her ministry has been committed to serving. I fully support The Felicia Young Ministry as she continues her work to change the lives of many people who have struggled to overcome their addictions and find God." Touch Down from Heaven reflects that.

Shawn & Rhonda McLemore

God allowed us to meet Ms. Felicia Young through a mutual friend. When we met her, we instantly knew that she is Ministry driven. Ms. Young poured out her heart and explained to us the vision that God had given her. One would be the book entitled "Touchdown from Heaven". We wanted to know how could we help her and that was through the cd that was produced through her vision. She allowed people of God that has a heart to Minister but didn't have the contacts or ways to get it done. The cd has blessed many people and we stand in agreement with Ms.Young that this book will touch many lives and give hope to the hopeless. She's a walking testimony of what happens when you totally sell out and allow God to show Himself Mighty in your life. She is Felicia Young the mother of Vince Young but she is the tool that God has placed in this world to help parents to understand you may have to go through the fire but stay in the Will of God and he will bless your life, your kid's life, your grandkids life and everyone that is attached to you.

We salute you Ms. Felicia Young on a job well done with this book and cd.

Felecia Matthews
NFL Mother of former Detroit Lions Will Matthews

Ms. Felicia Young not only brings us hope and inspiration but takes one on a lifes journey that's on point and down to earth. This book embrasses day to day experiences on just how real life is for people all over the world. Life through her eyes reflects the love God has for us and His awesome attempt to reach and touch as many people as possible with the good news that His loving kindness is better than life. ~Felecia Matthews~

Bishop Samuel L. Williams

Ephesians 4:11-12 states "And he gave some, Apostles; and some, Prophets; and some, Evangelist; and some, Pastors and Teachers. :for the perfecting of the saints, for the work of the ministry, for the edifying of the body of CHRIST. Of all of these callings there is none more essential to the kingdom, for such a time as this as Evangelism. Gods Touch Down is hands down one of the best tools for any one that needs a manual to supplement their ministry with material that can "Touch The Soul Of Man. Ms. Lisa has allowed Herself to be transparent to the point of being vulnerable to the hand of some that may not understand her purpose in revealing the core of her intimate and personal experiences. But that fact alone is the anointing of the text. For, it is only when the truth is told, that truth can be revealed. Felicia Young is on the evangelistic trail with her Bible in her hand, tucked under her arm and pressing toward the goal Line.

I can see her scoring all across the world as millions will read this Text and ask the Question, "What Must I do the be saved", Believing that GOD has changed her, surely he can do the same for them.

I offer this testament in Love, because, "GOD is the greatest Power!"

Bishop Sam Williams
New Gospel Experience Ministries
Bronx, New York

ACKNOWLEDGEMENTS

I have to first acknowledge Antoinette Latham who started out with me first in putting my testimony and vision from God together. She is also responsible for the ghostwriting of this book. Thank you Antoinette.

I acknowledge Chandra Taylor, Author and Writer, who selfless stood by me to see this book edited and completed. She also encouraged me to pursue what God had given to me to tell to the readers of this book. Thank you Chandra.

I recognize my Pastor, Samuel H. Smith who by an example of a faith walker, street evangelist of all time, a true servant of the Lord, who is after God's own heart, who also taught me to walk upright, wholeheartly, blameless, and to be fair in my dealings in all things. Thank You Pastor.

I offer my tribute to the Felicia Young Ministry team: Kenneth & Audrey Young, Matthew & Rose Vallie, Alma Huff, James Taylor, Rev. Lemuel Moton and my sisters & bothers who labor with me in the body of Christ. Thank You.

I also have to recognize the business side; Elton Lockings at Law, Reginald Patrick- Accountant, Bishop Sam Williams-GMWA, Pastor Greg Patrick, Chris Clark, Yvette Adams, Visual Connection-Varoy & Patrica Davis, Ken Nutt-Global Graffiti, Inc. Thank y'all for allowing God to use your resources to put what was needed to bring the ministry into action.

I appreciate and recognize my Son Vincent Young Jr., who loved me enough to support me with his monetary gifts. "He got it like that…", which was also a called from God to greatly bless me through my Son Vincent. Thank You Son for being obedient to the called.

I appreciate my sister Congresswoman Sheila Jackson Lee and her staff, who no matter where she is, even while beating down the doors of

Washington for the people cause, she still finds the time to support, to encourage, to listen, and to be a true friend. Thank you Sheila. Along with Mrs. Elyse Lanier, since the day I met her, she have always shown kindness and friendship to this entire family. Thank you Mrs. Elyse and Mayor Bob Lanier.

To my prayer warriors- Pastor Samuel H. Smith and Silver Smith, Mt. Hored Family, Rev. Bill and Nicole Brown, Shawn & Rhonda McLemore, Bishop Sam Williams, Felecia Matthews and family, the Vallie Family, The Young Family, The Wynne Family, Rev. Ed Malone and Sunday School Teacher for Women- Sis. Edna Malone, Professional Football Players Mother's Association, and my senior Missions Sisters, I thank God for the prayers of the righteous availed much. Thank You.

Most importantly, first and foremost, all Praises go to You, God the Father, God, the Son, Jesus Christ, God the Holy Spirit, this book would be nothing if you had not save my life for all eternity. Thank You, Whom all blesses flow.

I Love You, Lord.

A Message from the Author

Please enjoy my first book entitled *Touchdown from Heaven*. It is by the direction of God, My Lord and Savior, that I replay my past to tell this story. I want to share my life with you. This is not written to air my dirty laundry, have you feel sorry for me, or for you to be judgmental. It is written to encourage you and give you hope for your future.

I just truly want you to know that with God *all* things are possible. No matter what your past or current circumstances may be, you can have peace and joy in Christ Jesus. I am not saying that you won't have any more trials and tribulations, but what I can assure you is that you can have peace in the midst of a storm.

As you sit on the sideline and take a look into my game of life, reflect upon your own and know there is hope and restoration available to you as well.

Love to all,
Ms. Lisa

Table of Contents

Preface

Since you've decided to read this book, welcome to the team! God told me to tell my story, so He's appointed me the team captain of this game. Let me share the rules of the game, and then I'll meet you in the locker room:

Rule 1: Don't just read and be a spectator, be a fan of the Word of God.

Rule 2: Since we are teammates, you will discover this book is as much about you as it is about me.

Rule 3: It is my desire that through this book you will discover and experience the true love of God.

Rule 4: Allow your faith to be increased and learn from my personal experiences.

Rule 5: As you use the study guide, please take the time to create your playbook to victory.

In the Locker Room

This is where we get ready for the game, so put on your armor of God because we might get beat up when we go out there on the battlefield. The enemy is waiting. When we are in the huddle, I'll share with you my story. We will have some sideline chats because there are some things I just want to talk about and I need to make sure you understand. And lastly, I want you to take the time to apply the game plan to your life.

Every victory begins with prayer. Let us pray.

Pre-Game Prayer
Psalm 71:1–24

In thee, O LORD, do I put my trust: let me never be put to confusion
Deliver me in thy righteousness, and cause me to escape:
incline thine ear unto me, and save me.
Be thou my strong habitation, whereunto I may continually resort: thou hast
given commandment to save me; for thou art my rock and my fortress.
Deliver me, O my God, out of the hand of the wicked, out
of the hand of the unrighteous and cruel man
For thou art my hope, O Lord GOD: thou art my trust from my youth.
By thee have I been holden up from the womb: thou art he that took me
out of my mother's bowels: my praise shall be continually of thee
I am as a wonder unto many; but thou art my strong refuge
Let my mouth be filled with thy praise and with thy honour all the day
Cast me not off in the time of old age; forsake me not when my strength faileth.
For mine enemies speak against me; and they that lay
wait for my soul take counsel together
Saying, God hath forsaken him: persecute and take
him; for there is none to deliver him.
O God, be not far from me: O my God, make haste for my help.
Let them be confounded and consumed that are adversaries to my soul;
let them be covered with reproach and dishonour that seek my hurt
But I will hope continually, and will yet praise thee more and more
My mouth shall shew forth thy righteousness and thy salvation
all the day; for I know not the numbers thereof
I will go in the strength of the Lord GOD: I will make
mention of thy righteousness, even of thine only.
O God, thou hast taught me from my youth: and
hitherto have I declared thy wondrous works.
Now also when I am old and greyheaded, O God, forsake me
not; until I have shewed thy strength unto this generation,
and thy power to every one that is to come.
Thy righteousness also, O God, is very high, who hast
done great things: O God, who is like unto thee!
Thou, which hast shewed me great and sore troubles, shalt quicken me
again, and shalt bring me up again from the depths of the earth.
Thou shalt increase my greatness, and comfort me on every side
I will also praise thee with the psaltery, even thy truth, O my God:
unto thee will I sing with the harp, O thou Holy One of Israel.
My lips shall greatly rejoice when I sing unto thee;
and my soul, which thou hast redeemed.
24My tongue also shall talk of thy righteousness all the day long: for they
are confounded, for they are brought unto shame, that seek my hurt.
In the name of Jesus. Amen!
This is my prayer.

We are prayed up; now let's suit up in the Word!

The Armor of God

Ephesians 6:10–18

"Be strong in the Lord and in the power of His might. Put on the whole armor of God that you may be able to stand against the wiles of the devil. For we do not wrestle against flesh and blood, but against principalities, against powers, against the rulers of the darkness of this age, against spiritual hosts of wickedness in the high place.

"Wherefore take onto you the whole armor of God, that ye may be able to withstand in the evil day, and having done all, to stand. Stand therefore, having your loins grit about with truth, and having on the breastplate of righteousness, and your feet shod with the preparation of the gospel of peace; above all, taking the shield of faith, wherewith ye shall be able to quench all the fiery darts of the wicked.

"And take the helmet of salvation, and the sword of the Spirit, which is the Word of God; praying always with all prayer and supplication in the Spirit, watching thereunto with all perseverance and supplication for all saints;"

PARTS OF ARMOR	KNOW THE TRUTH ABOUT...	AFFIRM KEY SCRIPTURES
Belt of TRUTH	God	Deuteronomy 4:39; Psalm 23:1; 18:1–3
Breastplate of RIGHTEOUSNESS	The Righteousness of Jesus in you	Psalm 100:3; Rom. 3:23–24, 6:23; Galatians 2:20–21; Philippians. 3:8–10
Sandals of PEACE	Inner peace and readiness	Romans 5:1; Ephesians 2:14; John 14:27, 16:33, 20:21
Shield of FAITH	Living by faith	Romans 4:18–21; Hebrews 11:1; 1 Peter 1:6–7
Helmet of SALVATION	Salvation through Christ today and forever	Psalm 16: 23; Hebrews 1:3–6; 2 Corinthians 4:16–18; 1 Thessalonians 4:17; 1 John 3:1–3
Sword of the Spirit GOD'S WORD	God's Word countering spiritual deception and accusations	Hebrews 4:12; Matthew 4:2–11; 1 Peter 3:15; Psalm 119:110–112

Chapter 1

God Is Love: He **Guards** Us from the Enemy

"And we have known and believed the love that God hath to us. God is love; and he that dwelleth in love dwelleth in God, and God in him"
—1 John 4:16

"You cannot earn God's love. It's a free gift. "My unconditional love is given to all with no strings attached, free of charge." God's love is not based on what you do or give, God's love is unconditional." Ms. Lisa

In some very familiar Bible stories, Jesus tells about a shepherd who left His ninety-nine sheep and found the missing one. He tells about a woman who lost one of her ten coins and looked for it. He tells about a prodigal son who leaves home and spends all he has. When he comes home his father welcomes him. God loves sinners not the sin (Luke 15:1–33).

In the Huddle

This story is told by a converted woman who always had the love of God planted in her heart. That's me. You can call me Ms. Lisa. My grandparents told me as a young girl, "Child, you gotta have God stored in your heart!" God is love! I never knew what that meant until now.

My first love lesson came from my grandparents, Eliza Owens and Smith Owens. My grandparents were my rock! I can honestly say they were the best coaches I've ever had. Their love was not just lip service. They showed it. I mean they did everything for everybody. If Ms. Loula was sick; you best believe we would be taking over a casserole. If Mr. Wiley needed a ride to church, he could count on Granddaddy, and if

Sister Dora needed help with the church banquet, Grandma was there. I really believe this is from where I got my giving spirit. I always saw them giving and doing for others, so giving is definitely a part of my roots. They planted seeds in my life from which I am now receiving a harvest. I remember when we'd sit at the table for breakfast and dinner; my granddaddy would bless the food by saying the entire twenty-third Psalm. Now I understand the true meaning of the "Lord is my Shepherd, I shall not want." My grandparents loved God's way, unconditionally and unselfishly. I never really knew what that meant until now. God is love! God's love is unconditional. Have you ever really thought about what that means? God is everything, and love is eternal. What does love mean to us, when we say we love is conditional.

Sideline Chat

It's important to have Godly love. When you have Godly love, your love is unselfish and unconditional. Are you guilty of loving someone because of what they have, how they look, or what they can do for you? Answer the question honestly. If this is how you love, then your love is conditional and you will never be fulfilled in this area of your life. That's why there are so many broken relationships, because we base our love on conditions, like "she use to look good, but now she's gained too much weight," or "he doesn't excite me anymore," or "she is nagging me too much," or "he's not a superstar anymore and I can't shop like I used to." You get my drift! My advice to you is before you commit to someone, examine the premise of your love and make sure God is the foundation. You can't help how others treat you, but you can definitely control how you treat others.

Another important lesson about love: you cannot receive God's reward if you harbor jealousy and bitterness in your heart. Let it go. Don't be mad at the 'Joneses because they have a big house, fine cars, and appear to have it going on. I say *appears* because I know so many people—and I have been in this place myself—where it looks like we've got it going on, but inside our homes and our hearts, all hell is breaking loose. Don't be deceived.

Many of you may be guilty of exalting yourselves, but the real blessing is when God exalts us. When you are self-exalted, you break lots of hearts and step on many people's toes and heads, and God is not pleased. In reality you are not on a firm foundation and things will come tumbling down. When God exalts you, He will make your enemies your footstool. Don't believe me? Read Psalm 110:1.

You see, team, God judges our hearts. We may be on different levels of our spiritual journey, but God knows our intentions and our desires to do well, so just because someone is a Bible-totin', scripture-quotin', I-know-God-better-than-you saint, this does not mean God loves them more or will do more for them. Often it's the opposite. God uses people who are willing to be used by Him and whose bodies are available and who will exalt Him and not themselves.

In the Huddle

What I want you to know, team, is that God is Love. He loves us unconditionally, in spite of our wrongdoings, our circumstances, or our status. He wants us to walk upright the best way we know how, and I assure you He will order your steps the rest of the way. There is so much I didn't know about God when I began my walk with Him, and there is so much I'm still learning.

When I was young, my mom, brothers and I lived with my grandparents. I spent a lot of time with my grandparents because my mom worked all the time. I remember we use to walk to church every week, and yes, I had to go to Sunday school. My life was built on a firm foundation. I heard the Word at home and at church. I truly believed God was with me, and I gave my life to Christ when I was nine years old. I believed in my heart and I confessed with my mouth that He is the Son of God and He was raised from the dead, and on that Sunday morning I was saved.

I remember my grandparents teaching my brothers and me bible verses pertaining to life's journey. They wanted to make sure we had all of the instructions (the bible) we needed to survive this so called game of life. We stayed in the church house; I think I was more of a church fixture than the pew. We were in the church day in and day out. We fed the sick, transported the neighbors to and from church, to the grocery store, the doctor's office, wherever they needed to go. No matter what was needed, my grandparents helped and showed everyone love. This is where I learned to be a cheerful giver. All my life all I knew to do was to share with others.

Do everything in love. It's the basis of all things. God summarizes all his commandments by giving us the commandment to love. We are to love God, and we are to love God by loving other people. We are to be vessels of God's love to our neighbors. This allows God to demonstrate His love through us. All of God's Word is about love. It is about what love is and who love is. God is love. The Bible reveals love to us. It also reveals God to us. When we know God, we know love. God desires that we express our love to Him through obeying His voice. This shows Him that we love and trust Him, and it is the beginning of true worship.

The Game Plan: Reflection of Love

"He that loveth not knoweth not God; for God is love,"
—1 John 4:8

List three attributes about God's character that you love:

_____

_____

_____

Do you believe in love?

_____

_____

_____

How was love expressed to you as a child? By whom?

_____

_____

_____

How do you express love?

_____

_____

_____

Who had the greatest influence on you as a child?

_____

_____

_____

Describe what love feels like.

_____

_____

_____

What is your favorite love song?

_____

_____

_____

Have you ever been hurt by someone who said they loved you?

_____

_____

_____

How did you handle the pain?

_____

_____

_____

Chapter 2

Overcoming Obstacles:
When the **Odds** are Against You

"These things I have spoken unto you, that in me ye
might have peace. In the world ye shall have tribulation:
but be of good cheer; I have overcome the world."
—John 16:33

In the Tunnel

As we get ready for the game, I just want you to know that we will
encounter some obstacles. As defined by the dictionary, an obstacle is one
that opposes, stands in the way of, or holds up progress. So in our case,
that could be the enemy, our choices, or so-called friends on the opposing
team. Don't worry; in the end we will have the victory in Christ Jesus.

Sideline Chat

Now look, as we go into this game of life, I want to warn you that we
are going to encounter some things that will put us on our back, make us
doubt everything we were ever taught to believe in and make us wonder
why we even exist. In case you don't know God, I assure you you were
created for a purpose. Your assignment is to diligently seek God so you
may have an abundant life as you pursue your destiny. Don't quit. Stay
in the game. The obstacles in your life are there to make you stronger,
build your faith, and put you on the road to your destiny. I am a living
testimony. Join me in the huddle and let's talk.

In the Huddle

Let me tell you about some of the obstacles and life's lessons I went through to get where I am today. You know the saying "a hard head makes a soft behind?" I can testify to that! A hard head with bad choices can lead you down a road of destruction. I had a great foundation—thank God for that—but I did do some things during my lifetime that would not edify God. I'll share some of these stories with you. My grandfather died when I was nine. That's when we moved to Hiram Clarke, a nice inner-city community in Houston, Texas. My grandmother moved in with us to take care of my brothers and me. We lived what I thought was a comfortable life until my grandmother died and I had to grow up quick because Mama was working. I spent many days home alone taking care of my brothers.

I had so many things to happen to me when I was coming up, at the time I didn't know the reason for my destruction, but thanks be to God I have a clearer understanding now.

The Obstacle that Made a S.U.R.V.I.V.O.R.

When I was fifteen, I had one of the most devastating experiences of my life. I was a victim of a female's greatest fear: rape. My temple was invaded and my innocence was stolen by a stranger's aggression and need for power. The violation I felt is indescribable. I went into shock as I witnessed my brothers being tied up as I was forced into my mom's bedroom by this madman with a gun. He told me to "shut up and be still" as he stripped off my clothes and penetrated my body, which went limp. My heart sank to my toes, and I thought, *is this really happening to me?* I prayed that I would wake up from this nightmare, I closed my eyes, and then opened them, but he was still there. I closed my eyes again, rubbed them real hard, and opened them, and he was still pressed against my body. It was not a dream!

When he was done, he told me not to move as he shuffled through the bedroom drawers looking for money. One of my brothers got loose and ran out to get help. Hearing the commotion the madman ran out of the house. I don't know if he was trying to catch my brother or just get away. All I remembered was when my brother was running back in to check on us, he fell to the ground in the doorway as a bullet hit him on the side of his neck. I was in shock! Did my brother just get killed right before my eyes?

No one knew what was going on in our house. Our neighbors were outside at the time. And to them this was just a typical day in the 'hood, kids running around, playing. Well the madman didn't just stop at our house. He broke into someone else's house on the next street, but this time it wasn't just kids at home. It was a mother and son—and their German shepherd. He got caught by the German shepherd. I also remember hearing he got a pretty good beating by the son and dog before the police arrived. My brother was taken to the emergency room. Thank God, he survived this tragedy.

I became very withdrawn and scared after this attack. I didn't want to talk to anyone, and I was angry inside and would cry a lot. I remember going to the police station with my momma to identify the suspect. Yep that was him; I saw his face and relived the pain all over again.

The madman went to jail and I remember we had to go to court a couple of times. My dad came down from California to go with us. This was one of the few times I remember him being there for us. The rapist got out on bail because his family put up their assets for collateral. Believe it or not, he never went back to jail—at least not when it came to my case. His family sold their possessions and basically bought him a get-out-of-jail card and moved out of Texas. The attorney asked me if I wanted to go further with this and I could not. I couldn't believe someone could get out of jail after doing something like this. I just wanted this nightmare to end, and I blocked it out of my mind for most of my life—until now. After that I became a little hard — not taking no mess from any man ever again.

Sideline Chat

Rape is a sensitive subject and is very damaging to many people. I lived through that life-altering experience, so I am a S.U.R.V.I.V.O.R. —Strong, Undeniable, Restored, Victorious, Intelligent, Vital, Original, Renewed. If this is one of your obstacles in life, you are a S.U.R.V.I.V.O.R., too!

Believe in yourself and get back in the game. Go to the Coach's Office to get more resources on coping with rape.

Rape is not a respecter of persons. I've known cases where young men have been raped, too. This is the devil's way of imparting perversion in our society. Statistically a greater percentage of young girls who've been raped become more promiscuous, and young men often become very involved in pornography and sometimes repeat the same offense. If this is you, you can be delivered! Stay in the game.

A word to parents: please listen to your children if they tell you they've have been violated. Do you realize the courage it took for them to tell you? Please take it seriously and get your child help immediately. There are so many people living in bondage because Momma didn't believe what Uncle So and So, the babysitter, or her boyfriend did.

In the Huddle

As I reflect upon the time of my life before I was raped, I realize I've always been grown for my age, often having boyfriends older than me. I started at a young age looking at boys and doing little things to get attention from the ones I liked. That's normal, but as you get older you are more apt to do things that you were taught not to do. I am not blaming myself for being raped, but I was definitely out there more than I should have been.

Sideline Chat

If you are a parent, please be involved as much as you can in the lives of your children. Don't encourage certain behaviors by thinking that's cute or they're just young and they don't know any better. Teach them and correct wrong behaviors now. We should all strive to teach our children more than what we knew growing up.

If you are still a youngster, please, please, please stop trying to grow up so fast. You have plenty of time to be grown. It's okay to have friends and have a good time, but be sure in doing so you make choices that will help you succeed. Have the spirit of determination. Stay in school, respect adults, and respect yourself. Your choices will determine your future. I don't care what your background, or what side of town you live, or what kind of clothes you wear, you can be successful. It's a choice. I'll be sharing some of my family's success stories with you later. Believe in yourself because I believe in you.

The Game Plan

Parents and children, I encourage you to go to church, develop a relationship with God, and get to know His promises for you.

Weekly Challenge

Spend at least thirty minutes a day with no televisions or cell phones and talk or engage in family time together. Play a game, discuss your day, talk about the future, etc. I guarantee this will be a life-changing experience for you and your family.

Sideline Chat

Ladies, did you ever play that childhood game where you had to answer three questions? What color skin did you want your husband to have? What kind of house were you going to live in? What kind of job would he have? Come on, I know me and my cousins weren't the only ones who played this game. Well, on my fantasy island, I was going to marry a light-skinned man so we could have pretty brown babies. We were going to live in a big brick house, and my husband was going to have a "good" job. That was the plan for my perfect life. What did you wish for as a child?

In the Huddle

I'll never forget our girls' night out at the Red Rooster Club in Houston, Texas. That night I met this tall, light skinned, baby-faced brother who could dance! *This must be him, that's who I dreamed about as a teen,* I thought. As Frankie Beverly belted out "Joy and Pain," we danced the night away doing the two-step and swing out. Little did I know that this song would be a prophetic sign of our relationship? During our courtship we partied and partied and partied! If I knew then what I know now, my advice to you would be don't ever marry a man you meet in a club, because that's where he will always be.

Since nobody ever told me, I married him. We were twenty-one years old. I was a few months older than him. We didn't have the fairytale wedding every girl dreams of. We got married at the courthouse, but I was just as happy. I was in love and ready to start my family. My husband didn't have the same level of excitement, but I figured he would after the baby was born. Yes, I got pregnant.

And the way I was raised, if you got pregnant, you got married. He said he loved me, but he wasn't so sure about the marriage thing. I wasn't going to have a baby for a man who didn't want to marry me. He said he wanted his child, so we got married. I was excited and trying to do the right thing, and he was young and uninterested.

My momma believed you marry her; you take care of her, so I move out. That was fine with me. We knew we could take care of ourselves. My new husband had a pretty good job, I was going to Massey Business College and working, so I knew we could make it. Instead of a honeymoon, we put our money together to get our own apartment at Hillcroft Square. We even bought furniture. I couldn't wait to get our place fixed up for our new family. Unfortunately, it could have just been my place because I spent many lonely nights at home. This is not what I pictured my married life to be. As Frankie Beverly says, "Over and over you can be sure there will be sorrow but you will endure." Joy and pain. Ain't that the truth?

Sideline Chat

If I knew then what I know now… My husband and I were unequally yoked from the beginning. His mom didn't want us to get married because we were from different religions. We really didn't know each other either. We did not put God first, which allowed the enemy to come in and steal, kill, and destroy our family.

The adversary, the devil, is walking about seeking who he may devour (1 Peter 5:8). If I had known in the beginning of my young days that my life was going to turn toward destruction I would have made better choices. I'm sure every soul on the face of this earth has said or thought that. Haven't you? The devil has been tormenting and destroying people from the beginning of time. No one is exempt from his temptations or attacks. Thank God for Jesus Christ our Lord and Savior because with Him shedding His blood and dying in our place we are covered so we would have a chance at eternal life and have it more abundantly.

In the Huddle

On November 17, 1978, God blessed us with a beautiful baby girl. We named her Lakesha. She was the joy in the midst of my pain. I dropped out of Massey Business College when I had the baby. My husband was out in the streets—a married man, living a single life. He was not much help at all as a father. He did have a decent job, but I soon learned that his money went to drugs, alcohol, and gambling, not to his family.

Even though he treated us this way, I was still so in love with my husband, and I was determined to be accepted and loved by him. I wanted to be with him so bad that I started hanging out with him and indulging in his wild lifestyle. He introduced me to the pseudo-love of crack cocaine. We were very young. Sometimes I cannot remember the good times because there were so many bad times. We had no order in our lives. We really didn't know each other, and we fought all the time. We knew God, but we didn't pray all the time. We went to my husband's church sometimes, but we were out of fellowship with God. We just simply existed, going through the motions and doing whatever Satan tempted us with.

Well we existed together for seven years, and three kids later we decided to separate. I know Satan was determined to destroy our family, and we were letting him. We didn't get a divorce because I still had hope.

Sideline Chat

In any relationship, whether you are young or older, I strongly urge you to follow God's plan. Abstain from having sex and engaging in sin. Get to know the person first, grow together, and build dreams together that you may look forward to achieving. Why rush into something that you know is destined to fail?

I've had so many people say, "Oh he'll change, or oh she'll change after we get married. Don't be deceived. That person will become more of who they are. For example, if they go out all the time, they will do it when you're married. If they never give you an unsolicited compliment, you will not get those words of encouragement when you're married. If they don't have a job, an unemployed spouse could very well be a part of your future. It is not necessary to settle. I believe God has a perfect plan for your life and that does include a mate for those who desire one. But the Word of God says in Proverbs 18:22, "Whoso findeth a wife findeth a good thing, and obtaineth favour of the LORD."

Let me help you: Women, stop looking for a man. You are out of order. The Word says let him find you and you will obtain favor from the Lord. Do you know how powerful that is? With God's favor you can experience an abundant life. You will be set up for blessings and you won't even understand why you received them. But God does this for you, so that He may be glorified. The Bible instructs us in Numbers 14:8, "If the LORD delights in us, then He will bring us into this land,

and give it to us; a land which floweth with milk and honey." That is pure abundance. God's plan is for family, and when you marry according to the Word you have protection.

For some of you, this may be the first time you've ever heard this before. It's okay. Just get into the Word and know the promises of God for yourself. You can start this journey with God in your relationships right where you are.

In the Huddle

As a single parent of three, I still had to maintain a roof over my children's head. I had to work and try to make a better life for me and my children. There were so many days where I didn't know how we would make it, but God saw us through it all. As Vincent Jr. put it, he ate sugar syrup sandwiches, but only when they ate all the name-brand food, then I taught them to make sugar syrup so they would not be hungry. My oldest daughter became so frustrated with our lifestyle that she ran away from home, and my youngest daughter was at home maintaining and waiting on Grandmama to get home from work.

I didn't know it at the time, but God had a ram in the bush. He sent me a great support system. My mother and her cousin stepped right in and helped me with the children. My mother-in-law who knew that her son was not doing what he was supposed to do for his family because he was in prison most of their young life would help me buy the children school clothes and she always gave them something on their birthdays and Christmas.

At the time, I thought I had everything going against me: victim of rape at a young age, abuse of drugs and alcohol, a failed marriage, and now a single parent of three beautiful children Lakesha, Vintrisa, and Vincent Paul Jr.

I came to realize I needed to make some serious changes when I noticed that my own children started modeling some of my behaviors—hanging out with the wrong crowd, not going to church, and not focused on success. The odds were against me, but I was determined to overcome.

Chapter 3

Deliverance: Get **Drafted** into the Body of Christ

"Therefore if any man be in Christ, he is a new creature: old
things are passed away; behold, all things are become new."
—2 Corinthians 5:17

We are born sinners, and unfortunately we have to go through some hard
lessons and sometimes even tragedy before we truly seek God who is so
loving that He will keep His hand upon us and allow us to experience
these obstacles while He patiently waits on us to come to Him. As a
believer the way to restoration is by the process of deliverance.

To put it simply, deliverance is to be made whole. To be restored and
returned to whom God created you to be. To return to who you were
before all the stuff was added. Now don't think that stuff is just sex,
drugs, and alcohol. Your stuff could be your lying tongue, backbiting,
unbelief, lust, pornography, deceit, etc.

Deliverance is a process. It's not a quick fix. This is why we experience
so many ups and downs. We want God to take away the urge or the
addiction, but we don't change our lifestyle, our friends, or our behaviors
regarding the sin from which we want to be delivered. I know you've
heard the saying, "If you take one step, God will take two." There is
actually truth to that. God is waiting on you.

In the Huddle

God showed me my sinful nature and showed me what His Word
says about the matter. The Seventh Commandment boldly states, thou
shalt not commit adultery. God speaks about adultery in the Bible.
Exod. 20:14, Deut. 5:18, Matt. 5:27, Matt. 1918, Mark 10:11, Luke

18:20. Therefore, we must understand God is serious about this act of disobedience. I have had many men in my day, and I lived like I was not married. My husband lived a life with others, and so did I. We had been separated for so many years it felt like we weren't married, but in the eyes of God we were.

Every time I tried to get a divorce back in the day, other things always seemed more important and distracted me, so I just continued to live in sin. To be honest, I was just simply ignorant and unknowledgeable about the fact that my children were viewing my lifestyle and I was sowing seeds of fornication into them. I didn't know the principal of sowing and reaping. The seeds I've sown can come back in my line of descendants. The life of adultery was not a pretty picture. I had so many relationships you would not believe, and I always wondered why I could not keep a "good man" and stay in a relationship. I would change men like I would change a pair socks or panties. Well the day came when I went to God and asked Him to deliver me from adultery, alcohol, drugs, cigarettes, and some other ungodly habits. This is when He showed me His Word about my lifestyle.

Galatians 5:16 says, "This I say then, Walk in the Spirit, and ye shall not fulfil the lust of the flesh." Verses 19 - 21 says, "Now the works of the flesh are manifest, which are these; Adultery, fornication, uncleanness, lasciviousness, Idolatry, witchcraft, hatred, variance, emulations, wrath, strife, seditions, heresies, Envyings, murders, drunkenness, revellings, and such like: of the which I tell you before, as I have also told you in time past, that they which do such things shall not inherit the kingdom of God."

God let me know if I wanted to be in oneness with Him I was going to have to change my lifestyle. I knew that, but I was not all the way ready, yet. I had one foot in and one foot out. If I knew then what I know now, I want to go to Heaven and I would have entered the draft a long time ago. I'm so grateful God was patient with me. I've been celibate for ten years now. I have also prayed and covered my children, grandchildren, and future generations in my lineage with the blood of Christ so they will not reap the bad seeds I've sown.

Sideline Chat
So if you are like I was and have no clue what it means to reap what

you sow, let me help you. When God begins to change your life, you have to take an active part in the deliverance process. The process could take time so don't get discouraged and think God doesn't hear your cry or this Christian stuff doesn't work. God is all-knowing, all powerful, and omnipotent. He does hear your cry. He knows what you've done, and He knows the plans he has for you! But He may take you down memory lane and you may have to reap some of the bad seeds you've sown, so you will remember not to go down that road again.

I'm telling you because I know. I've been there and done that. I knew I was out of God's will when I was doing drugs, fornicating, and committing adultery. Remember, I was separated from my husband, not divorced, so every time I engaged in sex with other men, I was committing adultery. I suggest that if you've done things similar to me, pray so you don't have to learn everything the hard way.

In the Huddle

I was sick and tired of being sick and tired! I began to reflect upon my childhood—you know back in the church house with my grandparents. I remember people used to go to the altar for deliverance, I couldn't understand what they were doing, but Grandma would tell me, "Oh, baby, they just gettin' set free from bondage—you know, from the bad things they were doing." All I know is that at this point of my life, if Grandma was still here, she would be marching me straight up to that altar. I knew that my grandparents would not be proud of their baby girl if they saw me now. I had to change!

It was a Saturday morning when I went to TranCo, the neighborhood store, to purchase a few groceries. I will never forget that day! I wasn't in the church house, but I knew I needed to be at the altar in that line for deliverance because I had done some bad stuff.

The sun was shining so bright it almost blinded me. I had to squint to see. I looked around and everything was so beautiful. I had never seen the world this way before. I began to notice every color. The sky was so blue and the clouds were formed so perfectly I just wanted to reach out and touch them. The trees were green and the wind was whistling through the leaves like a song. God had changed my perception of the world right before my eyes.

As I stood in front of that corner store and witnessed the beauty of

God's creation, I felt really different inside. I looked at my hands and they looked new, and when I looked at my feet, I felt on top of the world. I knew this was the day that I was going to finally submit and let God order my steps. It was a wonderful feeling, and one of the most awesome experiences of my life.

As I walked in the store, this time for some milk and eggs instead of a forty ounce and cigarettes, I saw a few of my after-hour drinking buddies. They looked horrible. It was like I didn't know them, but I did. I began to wonder, *is that what I looked like hanging out?* Thank God for deliverance.

I passed by them and tried to smile. They looked at me and kept going. They acted like they didn't know me either. It was strange. I felt so out of place. I glanced over at the cold box with the beer in it, and I didn't have an urge or taste for it. I felt like "who am I?" I was still trying to take in the fact that I was delivered from all the stuff that had me bound for so many years. I actually went in the store, purchased a few groceries that did not consist of beer, wine, or cigarettes, and walked right on out. Wow. I'm telling you, God is real.

I was finally free and I'm still free indeed. The Lord says in John 8:32, "And ye shall know the truth, and the truth shall make you free." Verse 36 says, "If the Son therefore shall make you free, ye shall be free indeed." Jesus Christ has made me free from sin. He has given me a way out. The Lord is in the deliverance business. He delivered me from drugs, alcohol, cigarettes, and adultery. And what is so amazing about God is that He promises to do this for all of His children. The key is you must be willing to surrender and accept Him into your heart and allow Him to redirect your life. That day I felt like Dorothy from the *Wizard of Oz*. I went back home and I had a great day. I started thinking about how I wanted to tell everybody what God had done to me and for me. I was overwhelmed with excitement. I thought, *He's fixin' me—little ol' me!* I couldn't wait to go to God's house on Sunday morning to give my confession and share my testimony of what He had done for me. I was so anxious to tell somebody about our Savior and Lord who delivered me from the darkness and brought me into His marvelous light.

That night the Lord woke me up at 3:00 A.M. and I knew in my spirit it was time to get on my knees and pray. I thanked God for loving me and saving me. At the time I really didn't know how to pray or what to pray for, so I just began to thank Him for all the great things He had done. This praise and thanksgiving turned into a conversation with God. I just started telling God what was on my heart. I would pray out loud, and before I knew it thirty or forty minutes had gone by. You are talking about a wonderful feeling, to be in the presence of the Lord. This was the beginning of my prayer life that changed my life. I am a living witness that prayer changes things. To this day God still wakes me up in the wee hours of the morning to pray for certain things and people, and I faithfully and consistently get up in obedience.

The Word says in 1 Samuel 15:22, obedience is better than sacrifice, but I went through a lot as my prayer life evolved. I remember just crying out to the Lord to forgive me for all of my sins and asking Him to wash me white as snow. I truly wanted Him to restore my soul and give me a clean heart and renew a right spirit within me in the name of Jesus. I was so tired of not walking in God's will. I did know better, but I just wouldn't do better. I didn't want to go back to my old ways, so I stayed before the Lord in prayer. Sometimes while I was praying I would feel a little fear come over me. I would just keep on praying. I now know that was just the enemy trying to take me out of that place with God. When you start to talk to God, everything starts to happen. The phone starts ringing, you get sleepy, the walls begin to creak, the sound of an old motor truck flies down the street and you can feel the vibration. It could have just been someone going to work at that hour, but it just seems to always be during my prayer time.

Then my mind would really play tricks on me, and out of the corner of my eye, I would see the shadow of a black hooded outfit that resembled the ones priests wore. I would never see a face or eyes, just a shadow of something black. The presence of evil was still trying to hang around me. It didn't feel like a right spirit, and I just prayed through it. At that point I would pray with the lights on, which would give me a sense of security. It would be just enough to keep me from being fearful while I was praying. Second Timothy 1:7 says, "For God has not given us the spirit of fear; but of power, and of love, and of a sound mind." Know that the Lord will not let anything happen to you while you pray, because He says the gates of hell will not prevail against the church. This is a lesson I had to learn, and I rebuked the spirit of fear and replaced it with faith.

Sideline Chat

One of the reasons we can't walk in total oneness with the Lord is because we still have some things in the flesh we can't let go of. Don't be afraid of being alone and of what people might say if you don't do worldly things. Stand up for what you believe in. I promise God will honor that. More importantly, He promises He will honor your obedience. Since I have been delivered, it matters so much more to me what God rather than people thinks. It is also very freeing not to worry about pleasing others and doing things you really don't believe in. I encourage you to take the 21-Day Challenge I will share with you in the Game Plan. Let me warn you the devil (enemy) will bring up everything you've ever done and everyone you've done it with, and I'm not just talking about sex. I'm talking about lying, cheating, smoking, drinking, back-biting, gossiping, you know what I mean—anything you don't want to remember you've done. I'm a living witness, when I was first going through the deliverance process in my life, the enemy brought up every man from my past. Even the ones I had completely forgotten about.

Luke 11:24–26 (If you read this in your Bible and the writing is in red, these are the Words of Jesus) reads, "When the unclean spirit is gone out of a man, he walketh through dry places, seeking rest; and finding none, he saith, I will return unto my house whence I came out. And when he cometh, he find it swept and garnished. Then goeth he, and taketh to him seven other spirits more wicked than himself; and they enter in, and dwell there: and last state of that man is worse than the first." This is so important that Jesus repeats it in Matthew 12:43–45, which says "When the unclean spirit is gone out of a man, he walketh through dry places, seeking rest and findeth none. Then he saith, I will return until my house from whence I came out; and when he is come, he findeth it empty, swept, and garnished. Then goeth he, and taketh with himself seven other spirits more wicked than himself, and they enter in and dwell there: and the last state of that man is worst than the first. Even so shall it be also unto this wicked generation." In this passage Jesus was describing the attitude of the nation of Israel and religious leaders in particular, just cleaning up one's life without filling it with God, which leaves plenty of room for Satan to re-enter.

The only ammunition the enemy has is your past. But the Word of God in Acts 3:19 says, "Repent ye therefore, and be converted, that your sins may be blotted out, when the times of refreshing shall come from the presence of the Lord." To blot out is to remove every spot, stain, or blemish, and to refresh is to make new, reinvigorate. God is clearly saying, no matter what your sin is, if you repent, turn from your old ways and convert to the ways of God

He will restore you to the likeness of Him, and you will get a fresh new start.

Now who would you rather serve the one who torments and tempts you, makes you think you are worthless, and keeps you in bondage because of the mistakes you made, or your Creator who promises His sons and daughters' forgiveness, restoration, and a life of abundance if we commit to His ways? God is not asking you to be perfect. He is the only one without spot or wrinkle, but He does want us to live a life of righteousness and obedience. Choose this day whom you will serve.

I'll leave you with this from Deuteronomy 28:2: "And all these blessings shall come upon you and overtake you, because you obey the voice of the LORD your God." Now that's good news.

The Game Plan

I want you to understand this: The purpose of deliverance is to receive freedom from any hindrances in your life that would keep you from walking in the fullness of God's plan for your life and your relationship with Him.

21-Day Self-Deliverance Challenge

I challenge you for the next twenty-one days to do some soul searching and get delivered from the things that keep you bound!

Make a list of what has you bound that you want to be delivered from:

_____

_____

_____

Ask God to reveal to you what is hindering you from peace, prosperity, and reaching your true potential. Is it your temper, your attitude, your lifestyle, your bitterness, your unforgiveness, etc.? Try the self-deliverance challenge.

Chapter 4

Seeking God: There is **Safety** in Him

"But without faith it is impossible to please him: for he
that cometh to God must believe that he is, and that he
is a rewarder of them that diligently seek him."
—Hebrews 11:6

The Old Testament and New Testament words for *seek* mean to seek
the face of God, to desire, to examine or explore, to seek earnestly, to
diligently search for, to wish for, to crave, to investigate, to pursue.

It is not safe when you are out of the will of God. As you've read, I
spent many years of my life out of covenant with God, and I was clueless
about my real purpose. I know firsthand what it's like to seek God and
understand His instruction for my life. Stepping out of God's will is very
dangerous. You can be easily influenced to take on worldly behaviors
of the people you befriend and with whom you hang out. Of course
you don't know that until you start listening and obeying the Word of
God.

In the Huddle

On my quest for knowledge and getting to know God, I began to
read the Bible. I would open it and just start reading, maybe a chapter
or two at a time. At first, I didn't know what anything meant or what it
had to do with me today. Haven't you felt that way? I started praying first.
This is sort of how my prayer went: "God, you are the most important
person in my life, and I want to be closer to you. I know the Bible is your
instructions for life, but please help me understand what I'm reading
and reveal to me what you want me to know so I can grow!" Yes, it's

that simple. Once you give your life to Christ, you can talk to God just like that. Some people may give you the perception that you have to confess to man or kneel at the altar before you can talk to God. In my opinion those are just religious beliefs. The Bible says in Luke 18:1, "And he spake a parable unto them to this end, that men ought always to pray, and not to faint." Think about it: you won't always be at the altar or confession when you need God. You may be like I was at the mercy of a madman, or at the wrong place at the wrong time, or you may just be in a situation you don't know how to handle. It's okay to talk to God anytime you want and wherever you are. This is the most important relationship you will ever have. Know that seeking Him is just the beginning of the game.

Ticket to God's Stadium

Another place to get to know God is by attending church and bible study. Pray about where God wants you to fellowship and worship Him. Church is a great place to enhance your relationship with God because God has anointed pastors, evangelists, and teachers to teach the Word so that you may apply it to your life. How many times have you been in church and the pastor is teaching from a particular scripture and you say, "I've read that, but I didn't know that's what that scripture meant?" I've been there many times.

As you study the Word of God, know what you believe. As scripture states in Hebrews 11:6, "...for he that cometh to God must believe that he is,..." There are many false prophets out there. Have you gotten a knock on the door, and when you open it you find two people standing there with a little booklet asking to come in to pray with you? You might think, *yes, that's just what I need*, but a few minutes into their visit something just doesn't feel right. That's the Holy Spirit tugging on your heart because false doctrine is being presented. Please know what you believe, and before you let anyone pray with you or for you, ask for God's covering and truth to be revealed.

With that being said, I also want you to realize that God will send someone to speak to you as well. How do I know? Because he sent Reverend Bill Brown, my converted friend and neighbor, to witness to me.

In the Huddle

The more I sought God, the more at peace I became. I could really feel my heart changing. Bitterness began to leave me. I found myself not becoming angry so easily. I stopped blaming others for the choices I made. I began to find joy in spending time with my children. I began to see what the enemy was trying to do to me, and none of this happened until I diligently began to seek God for myself, not because Mama or Grandma said, but because I wanted to know Him for myself!

As I look back, I can see that it's truly a miracle that I came to know God the way I do today. But I know it also had to do with the foundation my family laid for me. Yes, the principalities of peace got a hold of me and I was doing worldly things for some years, but through all that confusion, God moved mountains to bring me back to Him.

Sideline Chat

Deuteronomy 4:29 says, "But if from thence thou shalt seek the LORD thy God, thou shalt find him, if thou seek him with all thy heart and with all thy soul."

According to the Word, God says you will find Him. It doesn't say the rich or poor people will find Him. It doesn't say that black or white people will find Him. It doesn't say that sick or healthy people will find Him. It doesn't say that men or women will find Him. It doesn't say that educated or uneducated people will find Him. It says you will find Him, those who diligently seek Him. Simply put, God is waiting for you to invite Him into your life. This is the perfect time to practice your free will. Seek God with all your heart. He is greater than any obstacle you will ever face. He knows the plans He has for you, therefore if you constantly seek Him; He will make the crooked places in your life straight. He is the only one who can do this for you.

Even if you were raised in a household that did not teach you about God, you are still eligible for the Heisman! Just start to seek God now. Run with all your might toward Him. Throw yourself into the Word, and catch up on God's goodness. He will greet you with open arms, and you can still receive all of the blessings that someone whose been serving him for fifty years has. God is that good! He just wants you to be in the AFC—Always Following Christ—or the NFC—Now Following Christ.

In the Huddle

The spirit of the Lord let me know that I was going to and have to stay prayed up daily because I was one of Satan biggest devils. I wasn't an evil person, but I sure let him use me to do some crazy things. I was always trying to please men, and men pleasers and wandering eyes were a sin and that's a no-no in the sight of God who changed my assignments and my associates.

I'm human, so yes, I still kinda tried to slip out every now and then. It was about a year after my deliverance. God fixed it so the senior mission placed me over in-home Bible-studies. The people I had to go pray with were homebound and couldn't go anywhere, so they depended on me to be there. I'll never forget, one Friday night I went out, and the next morning I had to go to a home along with three other mission sisters, the teacher, and the assistant pastor of the church. We had a bible lesson and we sang hymns and had prayer. Sister Robinson who is now deceased told me that God knows everything! I tried to ignore her, but she kept whispering that in my ear like she knew where I had been. I became very uncomfortable. I felt so bad—I even felt guilty. I know now that was the Holy Spirit convicting me. I decided not to ever go there or anywhere like that ever again, and still to this day, I don't go to clubs or places of temptation.

Sideline Chat

After my deliverance I asked the Lord what He wanted me to do. The spirit of the Lord said to go and tell what He had done for me. You know the old cliché no test, no testimony. Since I've had plenty of tests, I have plenty of testimonies. God said when I give my testimony He will prick hearts, open spiritual ears to hear His voice, and He will save and deliver them from their sins and heal their souls. This is the plan God had for my family, to tell the world and be a demonstration of God's goodness. He wants that for all of His children. I'm determined to live the life of Christ before others so mankind can know the way to go. I believe what God said to me ten years ago. I trust in Him, and I stand on His promises still today. Nothing will ever take me away from the love of God. No matter what comes against me or what comes to me, it cannot replace my place in God. I will do the works of my Lord and Savior until He calls me Home. To those who believe, you haven't seen nothing, yet.

I diligently seek the Lord for everything, and I let Him carry me through. I am safe in His arms.

In the Huddle

Romans 10:9 say, "That if thou shalt confess with thy mouth the Lord Jesus, and shalt believe in thine heart that God hath raised him from the dead, thou shalt be saved." Lord, please, I confess all my sins and I repent all. I ask that you come into my heart and teach me how you want me to live. I believe you are the Son of God and that You died for my sins and paid the price for me to live for all eternity. Now make me whole so I can live and tell all what You have done for me. In Jesus' name. Amen!

Chapter 5

Turn and Repent: Get out of the **Trenches**

"Therefore I will judge you, O house of Israel, every one according to his ways," says the Lord GOD. "Repent, and turn from all your transgressions, so that iniquity will not be your ruin."
—Ezekiel 18:30

In the Huddle

After my deliverance I felt so safe in God's arms. I felt free, I had peace, and I had hope. But team, I want you to be aware that when you commit your life to Christ, the devil will try soooo hard to get you back on his team. Remember his mission is to steal, kill, and destroy. He will bring back to your remembrance every failure, temptation, and bad influence you've ever encountered. But one of the benefits of being a Christian is that you now serve a forgiving God. When you repent of your sins, God throws your sin into the sea of forgetfulness. Repentance will set you free!

Sideline Chat

This chapter is to help you identify the works of the devil and why we must get out of the trenches and turn and repent. The devil wants to destroy families, but God made us in His image to share His glory with us. He wanted us to fellowship with Him throughout eternity. He did not intend for us to be bound for Hell, which was made for Satan and his followers. God is about family. Satan is mad because our Father in Heaven has a plan for us and he was not involved in it. I don't know if you know it, but Satan was one of God's angels. He was the choir director, but Satan wanted to be more than God. He had too much pride, and that's why he got kicked out of Heaven along with his imps. Satan is a fallen angel. He's the prince of the air. Isaiah 14:12–19 explains how Satan has no power unless you allow him to have in control of your life. You allow him to have control by not having faith in God.

Our Lord and Savior stripped Satan of his power when He died on the cross for the remission of our sins. Jesus stayed in the grave for three days and rose again early one Sunday morning with all power in His hands.

You see, mankind was set up and bound for hell since the beginning of time when Adam and Eve disobeyed God by eating the apple from the tree of the knowledge of good and evil. They caused sin upon all flesh. Thank God for His everlasting grace, love, and mercy. That's exactly what we are living on right now.

Play Call

So, team, let me share with you a major play to succeed in the game of life. Repent.

What is repentance? The following six items come from Thomas Watson, a famous Puritan, who wrote about repentance. Please read this with an open Bible, so you can read each Scripture:

1. **Seeing your sin**—1 John 1:8, 10.
2. **Sorrowing over your sin**—we must do more than admit it. We must internally engage with it. Psalm 51:17; Isaiah 57:15; 2 Corinthians 7:9.
3. **Confessing your sin**—we must put our sin into words and agree with God that what we did was wrong. Psalm 51:4; Hosea 14:1–3; 2 Corinthians 7:11; 1 John 1:9.
4. **Being ashamed of your sin**—Watson: "blushing is the color of virtue." Jeremiah 6:15; Jeremiah 31:19.
5. **Hating your sin**—Job 42:5–6.
6. **Turning from your sin**—Watson: "Reformation is left last to bring up the rear of repentance. It is not the heart of repentance, but the fruit of repentance." Matthew 3:7–8; Acts 26:20.
   a. At the very least, this means removing yourself as much as possible from places of temptation (Proverbs 4:14–17).

b. If your sin was against other people, then you must go to them and ask their forgiveness (Matthew 5:23–24).

c. If the sin involves stealing, then restitution must be made (Luke 19:8).

Repentance is necessary for God to forgive us (Acts 2:38; 3:19; 8:22). Forgiveness will not happen until these take place. If we do not repent we will perish (Luke 13:1–5).

After my deliverance and repentance, I had to get back in church because I knew this was a place that would hold me accountable, and it was my safe haven from temptation.

My mom, my children, and I went to Mt. Horeb Missionary Baptist Church, receiving the Word from Reverend Samuel H. Smith. He's still my beloved pastor today. When I first started going back to church, every sermon I felt like the pastor was speaking directly to me. Have you ever had that happen? You've been out of the church for a while or maybe all your life, and you finally go and the message seems to be exactly what you are feeling or going through. You swear the person who invited you told the pastor all of your business. My friends, I'm here to tell you that's the power of the Holy Spirit. Have no fear. Surrender.

In the Huddle

Oh yes, I was in the trenches. I had to repent because I was definitely in the devil's camp. I want to talk to you about the biggest stronghold the devil had on me. It was Drugs with a capital D.

I started so early in life (fifteen years old) smoking cigarettes and drinking beer because my parents drank and my relatives smoked cigarettes. My auntie use to ask me to go and light her cigarette on the stove. I don't know what happened to lighters in those days. Well that little puff by the stove every day made me start craving nicotine, and before you know it I was sneaking to smoke my own cigarettes. Then, as the devil would have it, I got my first job working at Sears in the tobacco shop. I was selling cigarettes and pipes, tobacco, lighters, and fantasy pouches to put your tobacco and cigarettes in. I was making a little money so I started buying my own cigarettes, and I even bought my stepfather's cigarettes, too. This was just the beginning.

I coped with my failed marriage by drinking and smoking every day.

At first it was just a social thing with my partners. We would drink and smoke, and when we wanted a little high we smoked weed (marijuana). We didn't see anything wrong with that. We worked hard all day, so we needed to relax. When we had a hard day and the bill collectors were calling, and Calgon couldn't take us away, we even popped some pills. This took our high to another level and our minds to another world. But just like all addictions, this did not satisfy us, so we didn't stop there. As I made a little more change, and my husband popped in and out of my life, my posse and I experimented with crack cocaine, angel dust, alcohol, marijuana, cough syrup, and sometimes we had the audacity to mix it all together. We didn't stop there. We wanted to get higher and take it to another level, so we tried the rich man's high, snorting cocaine.

This killer drug was extremely popular in the eighties and nineties. It was the drug of deception. It made you feel like you had it all and was on the top of the world, and in the next hour you felt like the scum of the earth.

Sideline Chat

The world changed for the worst when the crack pipe was taken away and people started selling a crack stem—that's a glass stem where you put a piece of Brillo and burn it and put your crack rock on it and smoke it like a cigarette. The crack stem, smoking Brillo pads that you scrub pots and pans with, along with what they was mixing the cocaine back then, you would think destroyed the world. Pure cocaine was not pure anymore. It was a rich man's high, but after a high demand from all over the world, drug dealers started stepping on it, and it became anybody's high. It is the reason ninety percent of our families are destroyed today. Crack cocaine has affected families of every race. It's not just black people indulging in this deadly habit. It's present in every nationality. Smoking crack is a deceiver. You take your first hit and you get high, then after that, all you have is an urge for another hit but with no high.

Whoever you are when you smoke it, that's who you will become more excessively. For example, if you were a scary person when you took your hit, you will be scarier—scared that someone is watching you and scared that you might get caught. If you have more than a gram or have been smoking for years, you will become a crack addict. The taste and urge is a stronghold directly set up from the enemy. A crack addict is a

29

sad sight to see. I think Halle Berry's portrayal of a crack addict in *Losing Isaiah* is the most realistic. Crack addicts will not eat or drink water. They have to drink alcohol or smoke marijuana to calm down because they are so hyper. I've actually seen this with my own eyes. Some addicts get so paranoid thinking that the cops are coming, they will break out and start running like someone is after them or go into hiding. They stutter when they talk. Many addicts have strong desires for sex and like to have oral sex when they smoke. No one can possibly think this is how God intended for us to live.

Our men and women to start sleeping with the people of the same sex and became lovers of themselves. Satan has turned the people out with that same sex spirit. We are just like the people in Israel, always doing things displeasing in the sight of God. All people have to do is read the Word of God and they would know the truth.

Let's take a look at God's plan for sexuality as written in the first book of the Bible, Genesis.

> "And the LORD God said, It is not good that the man should be alone; I will make him an help meet for him. And out of the ground the LORD God formed every beast of the field, and every fowl of the air; and brought them unto Adam to see what he would call them: and whatsoever Adam called every living creature, that was the name thereof. And Adam gave names to all cattle, and to the fowl of the air, and to every beast of the field; but for Adam there was not found an help meet for him. And the LORD God caused a deep sleep to fall upon Adam, and he slept: and he took one of his ribs, and closed up the flesh instead thereof; And the rib, which the LORD God had taken from man, made he a woman, and brought her unto the man. And Adam said, This is now bone of my bones, and flesh of my flesh: she shall be called Woman, because she was taken out of Man. Therefore shall a man leave his father and his mother, and shall cleave unto his wife: and they shall be one flesh. And they were both naked, the man and his wife, and were not ashamed."

Please study the Word of God and know that sexual perversions are not inherited genetically but rather are learned behaviors and willful sins. Like alcoholism, drugs, and other such sins of the flesh, they may become very difficult to give up for those who have been enslaved by them, but God is able to deliver anyone who sincerely desires true freedom and salvation. Get out of the trenches, repent and God will set you free, and you will be free indeed!

In the Huddle

The people I hung with back then did enough to have a little money to eat good (a box of Church's chicken), have a car (Lincoln), go on a road trip (Dallas or San Antonio), and buy their rock (gotta have a hit). And we thought this was livin' large. The devil was setting us up the whole time.

No one in my clique thought we would end up with nothing—no job, no home, no family, no money, and for some, no teeth, no mind, and even no life. Many of us ended up back where we started—broke, on welfare, and in poverty. Even when I was on welfare I still could not get away from doing drugs. Satan sent all kinds of people around me with stealing, lying, lusting, cursing, wife beating, adultery, and lazy spirits. No one wanted to go to work except to make a little more money to buy more stuff. Not me. I went to work, repented, and turned from my ungodly ways and even from my ungodly friends.

Sideline Chat

Just think, after all of the years of abuse to my body I could have died of cirrhosis of the liver, emphysema, AIDS… I could have gotten killed or could have killed someone from driving drunk. Lord only knows.

Do you know how many people I know who are six feet under because of this nonsense? I'm sure some of you can probably name a few, too. It is only by the grace of God that I am free. If you don't get anything else out of this book, please don't ever think, *Oh, I just smoke or drink a little bit. I know how to control myself.* That's what everyone who has been and is addicted to drugs says. And I want you to know that's the trick of the enemy. He comes to steal, kill, and destroy, and he takes pleasure in doing it when you are at your lowest point in life.

During my time of restoration, a visitor came to my house. Reverend Billy Brown came to tell me that God said, "He has His hands on me." That day, I received and believed that word. If the Lord had taken His hands off me I would not be able to tell you what I know now. I truly received a touchdown from Heaven.

I have to stop and praise God right now for his unconditional love.

As I'm sharing my stories with you, I can't believe this was me I'm talking about. It feels like I'm talking about a stranger. I want to make it clear that was the old me because in 2 Corinthians 5:17 it states, "Therefore if any man be in Christ, he is a new creature: old things are passed away; behold, all things are become new."

Game Plan

As Ezekiel 18:30 states, "Therefore I will judge you, O house of Israel, every one according to his ways," says the Lord GOD. "Repent, and turn from all your transgressions, so that iniquity will not be your ruin. Make a decision to turn away from these ungodly ways. Confess.

Our Father in Heaven is so merciful and patient and loving toward us, the children of God. If you are living today, He's still trying to give you a chance to choose this day whom you are going to serve.

Are you going to keep serving the devil, the father of lies?

Turn and repent.

Sideline Chat

If anyone is still on that stuff and does not have Christ in their lives, they are dead men walking. That rock will have you up nonstop all day and night, and before you know it, you will be without anything—no family, no friends, and no funds. It is Satan's mission to keep people bound. Back in the day drugs were the big thing that had us bound, and most people ended up dead, in jail, or like me, giving their life to Christ. I still thank God every day for saving me. But now-a-days our teenagers are getting locked up and murdered, because we've let generations go by, and we failed to teach them and correct wrong behavior. We must stop this cycle of destruction.

With the war and the economic downfall, men, women, and children are in bondage more than ever before. People are losing jobs, losing homes, and killing themselves and even their families because they have lost hope. More than likely these people did not know God, and their faith was in their worldly possessions instead of the Word of God. Please, if you are in that place in your life, increase your faith—lean not unto your own understanding, acknowledge God and He will direct your path. He will make provision for you if you will turn to Him.

The spirit of the living God cannot live in your temple if you are serving Satan, the father of lies. Please accept Christ in your life and have a personal relationship with Him. John 14:6 says, "Jesus saith unto him, I am the way, the truth, and the life: no man cometh unto the Father, but by me."

Chapter 6

Obedience is Better than Sacrifice:
It's Not an **Option**

"See, I have set before thee this day life and good, and death and evil;
In that I command thee this day to love the LORD thy God, to walk
in his ways, and to keep his commandments and his statutes and his
judgments, that thou mayest live and multiply: and the LORD thy
God shall bless thee in the land whither thou goest to possess it.
—Deuteronomy 30:15-16

Our obedience demonstrates our trust in God who is our biggest fan

The main way we can express our love to God is through our
obedience to Him. This proves we love Him and trust Him. Okay, team;
I want you to know God is our biggest fan. He has our best interest in
mind and He wants us to win, but we must obey Him. He has given us
specific commandments in His Word to obey. Just like we expect our
children to obey us, God expects for His children (us) to obey Him. If
we don't obey Him, we will endure some consequences, and some of them
can be very tragic.

If we love God and obey Him, His commandments should not be
burdensome to us. First John 5:2–4 says, "By this we know that we love
the children of God, when we love God, and keep his commandments.
This is the love of God, that we keep his commandments: and his
commandments are not grievous. For whatsoever is born of God
overcometh the world: and this is the victory that overcometh the world,
even our faith."

Faith is the substance of things hoped for the evidence of things
unseen. Faith pleases God, faith is trust, and faith is love.

Sideline Chat

We are such an I-can-do-it-myself society that we try to do things our way instead of trusting God and doing things His way. For some of us, we end up like Saul. Samuel asked Saul why he had disobeyed God and Saul said in 1 Samuel 15:21–23, "But the people took of the spoil, sheep and oxen, the chief of the things which should have been utterly destroyed, to sacrifice unto the LORD thy God in Gilgal. And Samuel said, Hath the LORD as great delight in burnt offerings and sacrifices, as in obeying the voice of the LORD? Behold, to obey is better than sacrifice, and to hearken than the fat of rams. For rebellion is as the sin of witchcraft, and stubbornness is as iniquity and idolatry. Because thou hast rejected the word of the LORD, he hath also rejected thee from being king."

Saul lost the position of being king because he disobeyed God. His act of disobedience clearly revealed that he didn't trust God and love him completely. He was too busy trying to impress God and those around him, and he decided to do things his way, and it cost him his future.

What blessings or positions have you missed or lost because of your disobedience? God is not impressed by us trying to show him how great we are. He is impressed by us demonstrating our love for him by being obedient.

In John 15:9–14, Jesus said, "As the Father hath loved me, so have I loved you: continue ye in my love. If ye keep my commandments, ye shall abide in my love; even as I have kept my Father's commandments, and abide in his love. These things have I spoken unto you, that my joy might remain in you, and that your joy might be full. This is my commandment, That ye love one another, as I have loved you. Greater love hath no man than this, that a man lay down his life for his friends. Ye are my friends, if ye do whatsoever I command you."

God loved us so much He laid down his life for us, and in return He wants us to obey Him. After all, He is the one who sits at the right hand of the Father interceding for us. We have the greatest referee who will give of all the calls if we obey His rules in the game!

In the Huddle

Galatians 5:22–25 says, "But the fruit of the Spirit is love, joy, peace, longsuffering, gentleness, goodness, faith, Meekness, temperance: against such there is no law. And they that are Christ's have crucified the flesh with the affections and lusts. If we live in the Spirit, let us also walk in the Spirit."

I'm so glad I realized before I could obtain any of these characteristics of Christ I had to be born again. I had to be crucified with Christ. My sinful nature had to be denied in order to imitate Jesus. It must come from the heart first. My love for God and His Word made me have the desire to be obedient. Being obedient you will have Christ's love, His goodness, His faithfulness, His kindness, His patience, His peace, His joy, His gentleness, and His self-control. I receive all of these traits by spending time with God in the consecrated hour between 3:00 and 4:00 A.M., studying God's Word, mediating on it day and night, going to hear the Word in God's church, and carrying out His Word in every area of my life. You see, it has become a lifestyle for me. You know how doctors tell you to lose weight, you have to exercise and eat right? Healthy habits have to become a lifestyle. That's how your Christian walk is. You have to live God's Holy Word daily. It's the only way to live if you are a child of God.

John 14:23–24 says, "Jesus answered and said unto him, if a man loves me, he will keep my words: and my Father will love him, and we will come unto Him, and make our abode with Him. He that loveth me not keepeth not my sayings: and the word which ye hear is not mines, but the Father's which sent me."

In the Huddle

Romans 12:1–2 is a word from the Lord. I had to grasp these two passages of scripture. It says I beseech you therefore, brethren, by the mercies of God, that ye present your bodies a living sacrifice, holy, acceptable unto God, which is your reasonable service. Verse 2 says, "And be not conformed to this world: but be ye transformed by the renewing of your mind, that ye may prove what is good, and acceptable and perfect, will of God." This passage of scripture was used for my church's Women of Worth —Sister, Sister home Bible study. I was chosen to be an area leader for the South-Southwest side of Houston to make invitation to the unsaved, unchurched, and to believers rebellious and stiff necked and believers who were pressing on to the mark of a high calling, Jesus Christ. What that means to me is the scripture Matthew 16:24, "If any man will come after me, let him deny himself, and take up his cross and follow me." To be transformed in the likeness of Christ each time the Holy Spirit gives correction or the way to go, and then you must obey him. There were things in my life that I had to line up with the will of God. God had delivered me from drugs, alcohol, and adultery, but I still had curse words coming out of my mouth daily. I could not believe that I was delivered from all these horrible things, but my tongue still had me bound. I went to God during my prayer time and asked the Lord Jesus Christ to clean my tongue up. I knew the power of life and death was in my tongue, and if I wanted to speak life into my situations only praises shall come out of my mouth unto the Lord. I had to make a conscious effort daily to conform to the ways of God. Please don't think the minute you become saved and begin your deliverance process that you will automatically do everything perfect. It may seem like it's more difficult to do the right thing, but trust me that is just the enemy trying to trip you up again. You must practice laying down your ways and abiding by the ways of God. I constantly reminded myself of that acronym that became a worldwide phenomenon, WWJD—What Would Jesus Do? Whenever I wanted to do something questionable, I asked myself, what would Jesus do?

I stayed in constant prayer and I made time to study the Holy Word of God. It is so important to make prayer a part of your life. I truly know that prayer changes things, situations, and people. The beauty of prayer is that you can pray anywhere and anytime. You don't always have to be kneeling on the side of your bed for God to hear your prayers. You can pray driving to work, cooking dinner, or simply set aside some quiet time with God during your day. God is omnipresent and omnipotent and I keep denying my flesh to obey to do the will of God. I always believe we should live holy and acceptable unto God. For instance, I think we should keep the day of worship holy.

I remember my maternal grandmother always made sure we knew and did keep Sunday, the day of worship holy. She had cooked Sunday dinner and had done the washing, ironing, sewing, grocery shopping, and any kind of labor on Saturday. When Sunday came we would just worship and praise the Lord all day. We would fellowship with our sisters and brothers in Christ. Giving God respect and reverence was showing how much you appreciate that He loved us so that He sent His only begotten Son down from Heaven to save our souls. I know where He brought me from, and I believe He deserves all glory and praise from His child. Don't get me wrong. I know God allowed some people to work on Sundays, and that's for now. He knows when the day will come for you to give of your time on the day of worship. You can go to God in prayer about your days of work, to give you Sundays off, because you want to be a part of worship services definitely on Sundays. Ask Him to make a time for you on that day.

I still have some things for the Lord to work on, and I like to joke around a lot, and the Lord says we must be careful with our tongues in what we are speaking. If we can't speak anything good, we really don't need to speak at all. The Lord wants us to speak the things of God during our fellowship—no guile, gossip, wrong saying about one another. Don't get me wrong, the Lord is just as humorous as we. All things are made by God. To be transformed, you have to start your day out with the Lord in the early hour, which is three or four o'clock. This is what we call the early hour. When God wakes you up in the morning, putting Him first is, we go to the bathroom and then we get on our knees. If you can't get on your knees, then whatever is comfortable for you and the Holy Spirit, then begin to pray unto the Father. Matthew 6:33 states, "But seek ye first the kingdom of God, and his righteousness; and all these things shall be added unto you." It's time to spend some time with the Lord. This is the time that God comes around and fellowships with you like He did with Adam in the Old Testament (Genesis 2:7). This was also the time when Jesus Christ went to the garden of Gethsemane and prayed for us and Him before He went to the cross to die for our sins, the sins of the world, so that mankind can have life and to have it more abundantly and for all eternity. Also this is the hour of Jesus' resurrection. The time well spent is an hour.

Sideline Chat

By the time the Holy Spirit uses you to pray about the things that He places in your heart, you'll find yourself praising God, thanking Him, and asking forgiveness of your sins and praying for your family, neighbors, your church family, your job, God's people and their families, the leaders of our country, the leaders of every nation, the enemies and unsaved folk, unchurched folk, and believers who know Him that are rebellious and stiff necked, and the believers who are obedient servants. Also there's a moment when you just listen to the Holy Spirit. Then you pick up your Bible and study. Either you get a daily scripture Bible application or you can just pick up your Bible and just turn to the first page and begin reading. You have to stay prayed up from the time God wakes you up in the morning until you lie down at night. To be transformed is to line up with the will of God. There is so much in God's will, we just have to put ourselves on the backburner and do what God says, never compromising His Holy Word. You have to go and hear the Word of God. Romans 10:17 says, "Faith cometh by hearing, and hearing the word of God." This is the only way for you to be transformed in the likeness of Christ.

If you trust God, be prepared for Him to overwhelm you. Have the prayer life and boldness of the biblical character Esther, and let me share this strategy of walking in oneness with God with you play by play: To do His will is to follow His Word. This is an act of obedience, which entitles us to the abundance of God. This is receiving His blessing. God's blessing is what He promises. God has made the promise, but we must do our part and obey His commandments. If that means you have to change your lifestyle, change your friends, or change your schedule. Just do it. The reward is so much greater than that person, place, or thing that has you bound. If I did not surrender and turn from my unholy lifestyle, my family would not be where we are today. I had people praying for me. This was how God kept me, but it was my act of obedience that opened the gateway for God to come in and pour out His blessings upon us, and to Him we give all the glory. Just obey His Word and He will change your life in a twinkling of an eye. Is your disobedience hindering what God has for you?

Chapter 7

Understanding His Goodness: You Will Avoid **Unnecessary Roughness**

"Trust in the LORD with all your heart and lean
not to your own understanding; in all your ways
acknowledge Him, and He will direct your path."
—Proverbs 3:5–6

There were so many things that happened in my life, from my childhood tragedies to marrying a man who would not take care of me and my children. *Why me?* I often thought. I was good to people. Why couldn't I live the "good life"? What I have realized is that God was preparing me for the good life, according to His will. As long as my perception of the good life was distorted by worldly standards—drinking, partying, and doing whatever I wanted to do with no questions asked. There was some deep hurt hibernating in my heart for a long time. I have been tackled, sacked, and intercepted.

In the Huddle

Come with me, if you will, into this smoked-filled room—you know the one with the kitchen table, four vinyl chairs, and two ashtrays strategically positioned between two players. This was common place for me, sitting around with my get-high buddies' playing cards. That was one of my favorite pastimes in the hood along with drinking, dope, and men.

On occasion we'd step outside to get a little fresh air and talk to my neighbor working on his car. The little girls were out playing jacks and the boys riding bikes. That was my son Vincent Junior's favorite pastime. The minute he got a bike, he thought he could travel around the Southside. I had friends calling me saying," Girl, you know yo' son over here in my hood." He was only about seven or eight years old, riding everywhere, but he knew he'd better be home before those streetlights came on!

One day we were sitting in the house, feeling good, talking noise, and gettin' high! Midway through our domino tournament we saw lights flashing on our street. I wondered who they were coming to get. We quickly put up our stash and went outside to see what was going on. As my eyes adjusted to the bright Texas sun, people were running toward me screaming "Lisa, it's your son!"

What about him? I thought.

One of my neighbors Mr. C.J. said, "He was hit by a car."

My high immediately escaped me, and I started running toward the corner. My shoes went flying off my feet, and I got there in no time flat. My only son lay in the grass hurt—helpless and motionless. Someone called an ambulance and the person who hit my son left the scene. All of our neighbors were there. My son was scared and so was I. My mother took the girls and went home, and Vincent Jr. and I got in the ambulance along with one of my friends. Boy, I prayed and talk to God and asked him to save my son. God heard my prayer and He gave me another chance to be with my son. After Vincent Jr. was healed, Channel 13 news came to our neighborhood in Hiram Clark and after interviewing us, they gave Vincent Jr. a new dirt bike, helmet, and knees pads for protection. My little boy was an example of a second chance to tell other children about wearing their helmet and knee pads. I believe it was around 1995 when they reinforced the law of bicycle safety. He also talked to them about watching out for cars and what direction you should go and which side you should ride on.

At that time another direction had taken place in my life. I needed to direct myself and focus on my children. I had to find something to keep my children busy so that they could stay out of trouble.

Well after that, it was growing up time. There were so many things that happened to me in my life, I never thought that my husband would be one who did not take care of me and my children. There was some deep hurt hibernating in my heart for a long time.

I also had to deal with the loss of my brother who was next to me. He died in a car accident with a guy I had being dating for six years while

I was married. My husband and I had been separated for twenty-three years, but off and on we would try to get back together for the children's sake, but that still didn't work. Satan was still calling the shots in my life because it was destruction after that. I became harder in my heart.

My mother was still praying for my brother, my children and me. We joined Mt. Horeb Missionary Baptist Church. Over the years we went to church. My mother, Bonnie King, still prays for her children and grandchildren. I continued trying to find myself while the children were growing up. They kept getting into trouble at school while I was working and taking care of my mother, trying to be there for her and trying to make sure I had some time to myself so I didn't go insane. I thought I was going around in circles, not getting any farther in life. I worked as a home health aide, and I have always been a care taker. I had received my nursing assistant certificate after high school in 1975. I had work for University of Texas of Health Science Center for eight years. I had a lot of men in my life for friends and for lovers. I never had too many women friends because they did not care for me much and I did not care for them either. Women were so messy.

So as life kept dealing me ups and downs I was grabbing all the wrong things—other people's baggage—like smoking crack cocaine, which was something I learned in my marriage. My husband started me on that demonized stuff. I can't blame him for it because he did not force me. I just wanted to be with my husband, doing things with him. I carried that habit with me. The biggest set-up in my life was crack cocaine. It kept me bound. It kept me from moving up in the world, with better jobs, having a long-term goal. I kept getting farther and farther in trouble with that drug. It pulled me away from God. Before I knew it, it was nothing but party after party. My mother would keep my children while I ran wild, and while I was running wild my children were running wild. I thought my children were safe at home, but other demonic hindrances were keeping my family bound. My children were suffering because the quality time of a mother and a father was absent.

One time in my life I gave up my job at UT just to hang out with my so-called friends in the neighborhood. They were without jobs, and I just got tired of doing it—going to work and tending to the children and making good choices. I was hanging on by a thread. I was getting deeper and deeper. I had some bad company keepers who were nothing but wrongdoing people. My mother was living the life of hardship because my brother, my children and I were out of control. Everyone was going separate ways. The more she reached out to us, the more worldly things were pulling us away from her and home.

I started slacking off being out all of the time. I started spending more time with my children and watching out with whom my children were hanging out. The children were teenagers. They started running with the wrong people. I still had that demon on my back but was taking care of the children and going to work as a home health aide. The children started getting involved in school more. I got Vincent Jr. to agree to play little league football. I took upon driving Vincent and his little friends to Little League football. The coaches started to work with him, not knowing that my children had an attitude problem. They were victims of dysfunctional parents. My life had a new direction, the girls had their agenda, they were growing up and I had to keep up with them and their friends and the boys that entered into their life. It was tough. I had to talk to them about boys and the many types. They wanted to do what every other family was doing. They friends were sleeping over. I had to introduce myself to their mothers and fathers. Pretty much most of us at my age group in the neighborhoods grew up without father figures in the homes. We were all single parents helping one another keep our children and driving them, and we would put our food together and feed our children. Some of the parents were struggling like me. They either had men problems and weren't working, on welfare or had a drug habit and alcohol problem. We were trying to kill our problems with the wrong things. The devil would send men in our life and we thought it was a way out but it wasn't. It was the devil sending someone with some more baggage that kept us bound. The life was getting pretty hectic. I was trying to keep up. Not getting any sleep. I could not even work half the time because the children were getting in trouble at school or trying to leave school. Boy I did a lot of screaming in those days. I was somewhat like my mother screaming at us. What I did to my mother also happened to me. I did not know that while I was running the streets with God knows who, she was up all night waiting on my little brother and me to come in. That would be overnight. I would get in in time for the children to go to school. I mean I hardly ever got any sleep. Some days I would enjoy, but others I would pay for it. Days were passing, and we were at the football games in the evening at Vincent Junior's high school games, and Vintrisa was on the dance team.

My oldest daughter had run away from home by this time, and she stayed gone for a year. While she was gone she was helped by an aunt on her dad's side of the family. She eventually made a decision to go to Barbara Jordan School to get her GED. She found out by staying with her friend and family, she could not stay with them after the parents found out she had left home. At that time I did not know where she was staying. I had heard she had hung out with some of her cousins who were out there as well. Her aunt and uncle on her dad's side of the family went and got her, gave her some parental advice, and then they let her stay with them to help. I was very grateful to them for letting God use them to take my little girl off the streets and for leading her to finish high school.

She also stayed with her dad's mom and dad. Her experience with them at that time was a good seed sown into her life. She loved her granddaddy, Mr. Earl Young, who is now deceased. Mr. Earl spent a lot of time with Lakesha, telling her things she needed to know as a young lady. Kesha also received a closer relationship with Mrs. Betty, as well. By her going through that it made her very responsible and independent. She came back home and I was happy she did. I found out that when she turned eighteen she decided she was ready to move on her own. She and one her girlfriends and baby moved in together, which was another experience she learned while enrolled at University of Houston where she received her cosmetologist license.

Lakesha grew up. She was a hard worker, made supervisor at TGF Salons, and she then moved on. This time when she left she never came back home. She has been on her own since. I am very proud of her. She has all of the women's strengths on both sides of the family—the Wynnes and the Youngs. She's very strong minded, responsible, and independent. Also, she has a humble, sweet spirit, but as a small, thin frame. She is not scared of anything.

I had to put my foot down with Vintrisa and Vincent Jr. and told them about what time to come in and to get their schoolwork. I had to teach them how to take care of themselves—combing their hair and cooking, cleaning, and I taught them to drive. The children were all teenagers and I began to talk to them about how to handle themselves respectfully. I would tell the girls to carry themselves like ladies. Even though I did rough things I still respected myself. I better not catch them hanging on any corner or hanging in any man's car with Daisy Dukes on and their rear end pointing to the sky. I better not hear from any adult saying they talked back or cursed them or just plain disrespected them. You know that was a butt whooping.

There were chores. They had to know how to clean up and wash clothes. They had to cook a meal, they had to go to the grocery store and do the shopping. They had to be trusted to go and pay bills. They had to work a summer job. They knew that studying was the way to get out of the house and make it on their own. I told them we had no dropouts in our family. Everybody finished high school. They knew you either went to college or you had to go to work. The girls did real well about being good young ladies. Matter of fact, they were more responsible than I was. Vincent Jr. knew he was gonna have to be a man. He was going to have to know about cleaning up the house and washing dishes—I mean really washing dishes. You know how young men coming up leave water on the counter and the dish rag full of water? They don't like to sweep and mop the floor after washing dishes. Also they don't like to put the food away after dinner is over. He would take the trash out, just because taking out the trash was a man thing, he thought. He also was hardheaded. I would always have to get on him about his studies. He would easily get bored. He just wanted to play all the time and stay outdoors. I told them again that when the porch light came on, they better be in the house. Matter of fact; come in before it gets dark. If you can't make it in, you better call and let me know where you are. You don't go over to anyone's house without me talking to that parent so I will know there was supervision. These children gave me a hard time, but at that time the devil was busy keeping confusion going in the family.

One day at the kids' school, Madison High School, the news media was there and there was a disturbance and they were asking the children if they knew the Ten Commandments. Some said they knew thou shall not kill or thou shall not steal and lie. Well the newsman asked if that was all they knew. That caught my ears and eyes. I said, "Oh Lord, these people up here asking these children something that I haven't even sat down and taught my children or read it to them." I thought how embarrassing to me. I was guilty I had not taught my children anything. As soon as they got home from school I got the Bible and started searching for that scripture. I remember asking God where that scripture was. Believe you me, something told me to go to Exodus 20:2–19. That gave me the Ten Commandments. I talked to the children about what happened at school and I told them I had not taught them the Ten Commandments and I know that they had not been in Sunday school like I was brought up, so we sat down and I read the scripture to them out loud and I had them to read it for themselves.

I guess Kesha was about seventeen, Trisa was fifteen, and Vincent Jr. was fourteen. I tell you that was a beginning of a new life for my children and me. We started respecting one another and they started behaving and doing their work and they started setting up goals for themselves. We got closer. I spent more time with them. I would reward them with birthday parties and take them out to dinner. I would make them breakfast and their lunches.

After I found out what kind of food they were feeding them at school and that the children were eating junk food, I started making sure they were fed nutritious meals. Vincent Jr. loves hoagie sandwiches, homemade burgers, fried chicken, salads, and fruit. Kesha loves pinto beans, greens, spinach, tacos, and steaks. Trisa loves steaks, pasta, pork chops, cereal, and I would buy fried fish on Fridays. I would also barbecue, and I would make gumbo and jambalaya. They were fed and so was the neighborhood along with them. Vincent Junior's teammates were fed. My mom would be home when she was not working and she would be with us. The children loved to tell jokes and dance. They are so good at it. I loved to dance and we would listen to the old-school songs as they called them and played dominos and cards. We had a lot of down time. We mostly got together on Fridays after school or work.

Reading those scriptures changed our lives. Our family went to football games to see Vincent Jr. and his teammates win ball games. Times were getting busier and busier for us. I was working, going to the football games, and Trisa was singing and dancing in school. I was trying to keep up with her and Kesha who was going to beauty school. I was still taking my mother to work whenever or wherever, day or night. I was still trying to fit in downtime for me because I was getting out of control because of running here and there. I still was trying to keep up with those hardnosed people out there at the same time. Well, I started getting convicted while I was out there still doing alcohol and doing some drugs with my so-called buddies. The prayers my mother and the pastor were praying were working because I could not have any peace while getting high. I used to drive other people crazy because in the wee hours of the morning while still out I would start talking about the Lord while we were playing cards or dominos. They would start tripping saying I was blowing their high. I would tell them something was about to happen and I was not going to be there any longer. The day was coming that my life was going to change. These days were going to be over.

One evening my neighborhood buddies and I were in my garage getting high. A friend and neighbor—we used to get high together—came to visit. God had pulled him out of the darkness and placed Reverend Bill Brown into His marvelous light. He was going on about the Almighty Father's business and that was witnessing to His people about the Gospel of Jesus Christ. Most of my buddies would get up and run. They would scatter because they were too busy getting high. I would be sort of cautious about what I did in front of him because that was the respect I had in me. I would put away the drinks and drugs and give an ear to what God was using him to tell me.

The next time he visited was on a Friday evening. This time he delivered a message from God telling me that He has His hands on me. I thought, *what are you talking about, Brown?* I was giving a listening ear to what was being said. You know after that night I went right on doing the same thing. It dawned on me that if God had His hands on me then He'd been seeing what I'd been doing and hearing what I'd been saying. I was immediately ashamed because I was doing things displeasing in the sight of God. You know how we let things go in one ear and out the other? The next time Reverend Brown came he talked to me about our forefather Abraham—the father of faith, the obedient servant, and the father of many nations. God blessed Abraham to be the father of many nations. Reverend Brown told me to read the Book of Genesis about God's promise through the father of Abraham, Jacob and Isaac. I found out I was a seed of Abraham and there was a covenant between God and Abraham. What He promised him is the same promise God made to us. If you are a child of God, I would start studying a little more about His promises. There are about eight thousand promises that God made to us, and you will not know what is in store for you if you don't know His Word and His ways.

Well, as time was passing by, things were taking off in our lives. Vincent Jr. and the girls were working hard. Our lives were getting busy. Vintrisa was getting ready to graduate tops in her class from Madison High. She won a scholarship to Alcorn in Lormane, Mississippi. My family and I were always proud of her. She would always be the one to stay up and wait until mama get home from work and she would fix her bed, lay her pajamas out, and have her bathwater ready. She would stay up with her and watch their favorite show together until Vintrisa fell asleep.

If any of my children would be the one to stick with me would be Trisa. She was the one who stayed at home the longest. Even after she went off to college, she came back home because she was not used to farms and outdoors animals. She enrolled in University of Houston. She is attending college and working in her field, business, still today, she says she will always have a class to go to. She love to studied and gain her degrees.

Chapter 8

Commit to His Ways:
Make Him the **Center** of Your Life

"Commit your way to the LORD, trust also in Him,
And He shall bring it to pass."
—Psalm 37:5

In the Huddle

As life kept dealing me ups and downs, I attached myself to other people's baggage instead of grabbing the Bible. We fed off one another's problems and habits. This is how many of us get caught up and into trouble. We put our trust in things instead of trusting in God. At the time, I was introduced to some demonic stuff by my husband. I wanted to be with him so bad, that I did some of the things he did.

I was hanging on by a thread. I was drowning deeper and deeper in the pits of hell, and the Holy Spirit kept bringing to my remembrance, Psalm 119: 11: "Thy word have I hid in mine heart, that I might not sin against thee."

I knew right from wrong. What I've learned is that if you do wrong, wrong will follow you, and if you do right, right will follow you. I had to change what was the center of my life.

Becoming a Christian results in a changed life (2 Corinthians 5:17). A person will go from producing the acts of the flesh (Galatians 5:19–21) to producing the fruit of the Spirit (Galatians 5:22–23). This change does not happen instantly, but it does happen over time. The biblical character Paul tells us in 1 Corinthians 6:11, "And such were some of you: But you were washed, you were sanctified, you were justified in the name of the Lord Jesus Christ and by the Spirit of our God." When you are no longer in the enemy's camp you best believe that the devil is mad with you. He's mad enough to send all his forces against you. Here's what he did to me. First thing he says to me was that I was going to tell all that I had been doing and what God had delivered me from and people were going to talk about me and judge me. See, the devil was scared of exactly what I'm doing now, sharing my testimony and letting God's people know there is hope! I took a stand and trusted God at His Word. I refuse to let the devil use me again, and I share my testimony whenever and with whomever God tells me to. The enemy knows he cannot trick me again! I slammed that door in his face more than ten years ago. God is the center of my life!

Sideline Chat

Looking back when I was not committed to Christ, my life was like the Samaritan woman at the well. Like me, she was mixed up with the wrong crowd. She had been married five times and was living with a man that wasn't her husband. I wasn't married five times, but I had her beat on being with so many men, and I was still married. I was just sinning every day.

The story of the Samaritan woman teaches us a very important lesson, that we should not live by carnal pleasures and we should seek forgiveness for our wrongdoing. In the story the Samaritan woman traveled in the noonday, which was uncustomary because of the heat. But being ashamed of her lowly status and not wanting to be heckled by her fellow townspeople, she set out to get water for her household. Well once she arrived at the well a man was there waiting to offer living water, which leads her to salvation. Read the story in the fourth chapter of John.

The significance of the story is that Christ Jesus knows everything about each of us, but loves us enough to give us eternal life. He came to give all people eternal life, including the outcasts and those looked down upon.

Just Be It!

We must be a living example of God, not merely by our words but by the actions of our very being. When people are around us they should see Christ in us. We shouldn't even have to say, "Hey look at me, and I'm a Christian." Just be a Christian and God will draw all men unto Him. Just think, someone's salvation could depend upon how you live.

Having Jesus on the inside of you is unspeakable J.O.Y.!

Jesus comes first, **others** are second, and **you** come last. That's true joy.

You are rich when you know who you belong to. When you are last, you are first with God. In order to be like Jesus you have to be a servant. When you serve as Christ served you will become humble, and you will become submissive to God's will and God's way. Being humble will show Christ's spirit dwelling in us, and we will not be portrayed as meek and lowly. When we do things for God, we will be motivated and productive. Believe me, this book is a perfect example, when you are committed to doing something for God the enemy will throw every fiery dart he can at you! But he is a liar from the pit of hell! Just love your enemies and move on. I want to caution you to make sure you know who the real enemy is. The devil is the king of deception and he will show up as a wolf in sheep's skin, and before you know it you've followed him down the wrong path. Recognize your enemies, pray for them, and keep them out of your inner circle!

As we allow God in as the center of our life, we must begin to walk in the spirit and not in the flesh. You will know if you are walking with God because you will have a sense of love and peace in your heart. You will not harbor bitterness, hatred, or ungodly thoughts. Like the old psalmists sang, "Your mind must be stayed on Jesus!" If we want to walk in love and unspeakable joy we must commit our sinful tendencies to God's control. No matter what is going on in your life submit everything— your emotions, and your physical, social, and intellectual being—unto Him, and live the life of love and have unspeakable joy today, in the name of Jesus!

In the Huddle

This reminds me of the joy my family had when I committed my life to Christ and my sins were washed away for good. I decided God would be the center of my life once and for all!

I made my confession and gave my testimony, and I tell you that was the beginning of a new life for me. I praised God, and my children praised

God because they knew their mom was saved, delivered, sanctified, and filled with the Holy Ghost.

Our life changed drastically. My days consisted of taking the children to school and going to work. We attended weekly Bible study, and of course we were in the church early on Sunday mornings. I made sure I did not go anywhere out of the will of God. I was determined not to risk temptation, so I started attending Vocation Bible School. This was my first encounter with Jesus and the Holy Spirit. I'll never forget the first class I attended. The lesson was Fishers of Men. This is when I discovered my assignment was to live a Godly life before men and minister to them to win souls for God.

I had a dynamic Sunday school teacher. God used her in a mighty way. She told me to never go back out there—meaning back out there doing worldly sinful things. When Sister Edna Malone was ministering to me, I heard the voice of the Lord. It was so strong and powerful that I remember being scared. I knew then I was going to maintain an obedient walk with God, so I did not go back out in the streets.

Sideline Chat

Esther 4:14 says, "For if thou altogether holdest thy peace at this time, then shall there enlargement and deliverance arise to the Jews from another place; but thou and thy father's house shall be destroyed: and who knoweth whether thou art come to the kingdom for such a time as this?" Who knows if perhaps you were made queen for just such a time as this? Esther used her beauty and her character to win the heart of Persia's king. She put her life on the line by going before the king when the biblical character Haman gave a death decree against the Jews. We thank God for Esther. She fasted and prayed so Israel would not be exterminated. She was very courageous. She sought out a plan from God. She fasted and prayed for their life. If the Israelites had been put to death, God's plan to send His son, Jesus Christ, to Earth as a Jew could have been ruined. God's plans cannot be stopped. God had a plan for our lives.

Chapter 9

Hope: Let the Holy Spirit be Your **Head Coach**

"And hope maketh not ashamed; because the love of God is shed abroad in our hearts by the Holy Ghost which is given unto us."
—Romans 5:5

When you are walking with the Holy Spirit, your heart changes first, then your outer appearance changes. What you use to do, you don't do anymore. You walk wholehearted, upright, blameless, and obedient unto God, never compromising God's Holy Word for anything.

Sideline Chat

Someone is always watching you. In order to be used by God and do His will, your soul must be available for the Holy Spirit to dwell in. Before He put you on a mission for Him your life must be lined up with Him. There's a moment when you just need to listen to the Holy Spirit. Every team has a head coach who is specifically selected and appointed to lead the team. He is responsible for the team's overall actions. That is who the Holy Spirit is in our lives. When Jesus ascended into Heaven, He left the Holy Spirit to live within us and be our head coach. The Holy Spirit is our comforter, appointed and assigned to us by God.

We were each created for a specific purpose on this Earth. No matter how you were conceived, God knew you before He placed you in your mother's womb, and He created you for such a time as this. Stop beating yourself up about where you grew up, what kind of parents you had or didn't have, or what happened to you as a child. God is shaping and molding your soul for the change of your eternal body.

I'm just trying to get you to understand why it's important to let go of this world and let God have His way in your life. To be ye transformed is to line up with the will of God. Romans 10:17 says, "So then faith cometh by hearing, and hearing the word of God." There is hope.

In the Huddle

The Holy Spirit is your comforter and your guide. He will show you things to correct you and get you on the right track. I remember one of my first lessons in Sunday school was the story about the rich man and poor man named Lazarus. This story can be found in Luke 16:19–25:

"There was a certain rich man, which was clothed in purple and fine linen, and fared sumptuously every day: And there was a certain beggar named Lazarus, which was laid at his gate, full of sores, And desiring to be fed with the crumbs which fell from the rich man's table: moreover the dogs came and licked his sores. And it came to pass, that the beggar died, and was carried by the angels into Abraham's bosom: the rich man also died, and was buried; And in hell he lift up his eyes, being in torments, and seeth Abraham afar off, and Lazarus in his bosom. And he cried and said, Father Abraham, have mercy on me, and send Lazarus, that he may dip the tip of his finger in water, and cool my tongue; for I am tormented in this flame. But Abraham said, Son, remember that thou in thy lifetime receivedst thy good things, and likewise Lazarus evil things: but now he is comforted, and thou art tormented.

The rich man was in flames with worms coming out of his skin while burning. That alone scared me because I do not like worms, snakes, or any kind of creepy crawlers. Who wants to be burning for all eternity with worms eating you? That should make a person get right with God. It did me!

Well that passage of scripture made me think about and obey the Word of God. It also revealed to me that if you die without a relationship with our Lord and Savior, Jesus Christ, and did not have any love in your heart for others, it will not matter how much money you had or who you were in society and you could be headed for eternal damnation.

According to the Word, once you go to hell there's no return. And likewise, once you enter the pearly gates of Heaven you are there for eternity. Yes, it does take a lot to line up with the Word of God, but God knows your heart, and He doesn't expect you to not make mistakes. We are sinners by nature. He just wants to see you working toward the mark.

I found out that this was no joke, and I personally had a lot of work to do to line myself up. I am happy to say I've been doing it for more than twelve years now. Is it easy? Sometimes! Can you do it alone? No! Is it worth it? Absolutely! God's Holy Word is no joke. Once you decide to step over into the spiritual realm you have just gained a major enemy who is going to try to kill, steal, and destroy you in every way possible.

I know the Holy Spirit sent me to that class on that day to hear that story, to give me the hope and desire to live a righteous life bound for Heaven! Invite the Holy Spirit in, and let Him order the plays of your life.

Chapter 10

Decide to Forgive: Don't **Delay the Game**

"Then his lord, after that he had called him, said unto him, O
thou wicked servant, I forgave thee all that debt, because thou
desiredst me: Shouldest not thou also have had compassion on
thy fellowservant, even as I had pity on thee? And his lord was
wroth, and delivered him to the tormentors, till he should pay
all that was due unto him. So likewise shall my heavenly Father
do also unto you, if ye from your hearts forgive not every one his
brother their trespasses. This is how my Heavenly Father will treat
each of you unless you forgive your brother from your heart."
—Matthew 18:32–35

Did you know that unforgiveness will keep you from receiving your
blessings? Since God forgives us, we must also forgive others. God hates
sin, but He loves the sinner. Psalm 103:12 says, "It is possible for the
Lord to look at us without seeing our sins because when He forgave us,
He removed our sins as far as the east is from the west."

God's Rule on Forgiveness

Once you accept Jesus and become a believer, you become eligible to
receive God's forgiveness. If you repent and ask God to forgive you, all
of your sins are forgiven forever. That includes past, present, future, big,
or small. Jesus died to pay the penalty for all of our sins, and once they
are forgiven, they are all forgiven (Colossians 1:14; Acts 10:43). However,
when we stumble, we are instructed in 1 John 1:9 to confess our sins:
"If we confess our sins, he is faithful and just to forgive us our sins, and
to cleanse us from all unrighteousness." Yes, Christians do sin (1 John

1:8) but the Christian life is not to be identified by a life of sin. Believers are a new creation (2 Corinthians 5:17). We have the Holy Spirit in us producing good fruit (Galatians 5:22–23). A Christian life should be a changed life. A person who claims to be a believer yet continually lives a life that says otherwise should question the genuineness of his faith. Christians are forgiven no matter how many times they sin. We will not be free from sin until we die or Jesus comes back, but at the same time, Christians should live a more holy life as they grow closer to Christ.

In the Huddle

In 1990, I was dating someone for about five years, and through my relationship, my boyfriend and brother Keith (the one who got shot when I was raped) became best friends. We hung out together all the time. And of course they did the homeboy thing and hung out without me. Their hotspot was a little hole-in-the-wall on the south side of Houston called Nite Moods. Unfortunately, their partying days came to a tragic end on Dead Man's Curve. And I had to make a decision to forgive!

I'll never forget that night. I was spending the night with my cousin, and about two or three o'clock in the morning my mom came banging on my cousin's front door. She was pretty hysterical, and she woke me up yelling, "Your brother, your brother, he's been killed in a car accident." At that point my mind went blank and I didn't hear anything else she was saying. I was in a daze for the next few days, and we had to prepare to bury my best friend, my protector, my confidant, my brother!

I was devastated. Every time I thought about my drunken boyfriend killing my brother, I became sick to my stomach. The community was so mad at him. I was mad, too, and people wanted me to hate him, but I couldn't. He was hurting, too, Keith was his best friend and he would have to live the rest of his life with the thought of this fatal accident. My baby brother, Herman Jerod, has had a harder life since my brother's death. He was so hardheaded before this all happened, but he always had his big brother to chastise him. Keith would whoop Jerod's butt when he did something he was not supposed to in his younger age. Still today my brother is struggling with my brother's death and the separation of our father. Jerod was a young age when my dad left home around 1967. Today he has not let go the past so he can receive what God has in store for him and his family. We just keep on praying because he is a very intelligent young man and has the gift of a speaker. He has a calling on his life by God to preach the Gospel. He is also my mom's lap baby. You know how it is. I think the last child gets away with everything. They are the ones who are heavy on the heart. That story is a whole 'nother book. He would have to be the one to tell his own story. If he would go on and accept the plan God has for him, he probably would be that preacher of all times, giving his testimony to save souls for God who will set the captive free with this man's testimony.

Back to my boyfriend who got stripped from my life. As I was dealing with my own pain, I thought, if God forgave all the wrong I did, who am I, not to forgive him? Of course, we didn't continue our relationship, but I made the decision to forgive and I can honestly say I forgave him.

Forgiveness brings many benefits for those who decide to do it.

Sideline Chat

Okay, team, I want you to think about someone in your life you haven't forgiven. Do you have that person in your mind?

If you are not receiving what you want out of life or you don't think God hears your prayers, maybe it's because you haven't forgiven someone. We as sinners are not even worthy to not forgive someone. Nearly everyone has been hurt by the words or actions of another person. You were teased growing up, your spouse had an affair, or your so-called friend gossiped about you. I agree these things hurt, and it leaves us with a feeling of bitterness, anger, and resentment. In reality who is hurting the most? You.

Ironically, the people who hurt you the most are the ones closest to you—your spouse, children, siblings, best friends, or parents. I think it's more painful and harder to overcome when they are the offenders because it's someone you love and you don't expect them to hurt you. I want to warn you that when you remain bitter, small offenses can escalate into big ones and families and relationships can be destroyed. I know so many people who let people go to their grave without saying I'm sorry or I forgive you. It hurts them indefinitely.

Not forgiving will keep you bound to the situation or wrongful. Also, you will find yourself bringing bitterness and unforgiveness into other areas and relationships in your life. You will begin to create a very miserable life. If you do forgive, you will free yourself from this power and bondage and then you are able to embrace peace and love in your life.

When you forgive you decide to let go of the resentment and vengeance toward the offender. Forgiveness does not mean you condone, excuse, or forget what happened, but it will release the hold it has on your life. Forgiveness can be very challenging, and depending on what you have to forgive, it may be a process and take some time. That's fine. The important thing is that you make the commitment to forgive and pray for God's guidance. He will help you. You will be a direct recipient of blessings for your ability to forgive. Also, in an article I read, researchers are finding that unforgiveness and bitterness can cause long-term health problems. However, forgiveness offers numerous benefits such as stress reduction, lower heart rate, more friendships, greater spiritual life, lower blood pressure, better anger management skills, and fewer depression symptoms. Forgiving is a healing journey for your body and soul, so forgive for your health and well-being, too.

Chapter 11

Offer Praise:
You'll be the **Open Receiver** of his Blessings

"Bring ye all the tithes into the storehouse, that there may be meat
in mine house, and prove me now herewith, saith the LORD of
hosts, if I will not open you the windows of heaven, and pour you
out a blessing, that there shall not be room enough to receive it."
—Malachi 3:10

Praise God into the end zone. I guarantee you will not get a penalty for
this celebration. Your praise is the one thing God cannot give to Himself
and it is what He loves for you to do! You've heard the saying when
praises go up, blessings come down!

There are countless reasons for us to praise God. According to Psalm
150:6 states, "Let everything that hath breath praise the LORD. Praise
ye the LORD." That includes you and me. Praising God serves as a
reminder of His goodness toward us. Praise strengthens our faith, which
causes God to move on our behalf. Praise sets an environment of peace
and understanding.

It is clearly illustrated in 2 Chronicles 5: 13–14, "It came even to pass,
as the trumpeters and singers were as one, to make one sound to be heard
in praising and thanking the LORD; and when they lifted up their voice
with the trumpets and cymbals and instruments of music, and praised
the LORD, saying, For he is good; for his mercy endureth forever: then
the house was filled with a cloud, even the house of the LORD; So that
the priests could not stand to minister by reason of the cloud: for the
glory of the LORD had filled the house of God." Your praise will issue
in the presence of the Lord.

In Huddle

In 2003, I heard a Sunday school lesson about the praise of the biblical characters Hannah and Mary. The theme of Hannah's poetic prayer was her confidence in God's sovereignty and her thankfulness for everything he had done. Even Mary, the mother of Jesus, modeled Hannah's prayer as a praise song called the Magnificent. This lesson was so profound that I used this study as my own guide in offering praise. Like Hannah and Mary, we should be confident of God's ultimate control over the events in our lives, and we should be thankful for the ways God has blessed us.

Here's what I learned. Hannah saw God as a solid rock, the one who knows what we do, who is sovereign over all the affairs of the people, and who the supreme judge who administers perfect justice is. Knowing that God is ultimately in control has really helped me put the affairs and people in my life in perspective. I don't try to force things to happen nor do I force people to like me because I believe all things will happen according to God's time and He will send the people who will be a part of my life.

Sideline Chat

Even if you are going through difficult relationships, financial hardships, or feeling low self-worth, praise God anyway! I promise He will see you through because He promises to honor your praise. By praising God for all good gifts and life's challenges, we are acknowledging his ultimate control over our lives. The possessions and friends we work so hard to obtain will all pass away, but God is always present with us. He will never leave or forsake us.

Prayer changes things. My family and I stood on the Word as stated in Luke 18:1: "...And Jesus spoke a parable unto them to this end that men ought always to pray, and not faint." God has brought us a mighty long way. I know it was because of the prayers of the righteous. My mom stayed before the Lord on behalf of our family. Now that's one thing Ms. Bonnie will do. She will P.U.S.H.—Pray until Something Happens. The elders of the church kept us lifted in prayer, and my very own prayer life had gone to another level. It is amazing how when you turn from your wicked ways and live according to God's will, you'll begin to see and experience the promises God has for you. God knew when I was out in the streets the plans He had for my family. I thank and praise Him every day that He did not give up on me. What I hope you realize through my stories is that someone else's blessings may be connected to your obedience.

In the Huddle

I had to get my life together for the sake of my own children's destiny. My son, Vincent Jr., was an awesome athlete in high school. I'll never forget during the 2001–2002 high school football season he was getting a lot of media attention. He was in the newspaper every week during the season, he was on the cover of many magazines, and he was even being discussed in sports media circles. People were calling, coming by, and conveniently bumping into us when we were out in public. People were coming at us all sorts of ways, trying to give us things, but I was so in tune with the tactics of the enemy. I refused to get caught up in wrongdoing and risk my son's college eligibility. We had to be stronger in our prayer life than ever before. By us being the new kids on the block we didn't know who to believe, so we prayed every time we had a meeting with the college coaches and scouts. It did not matter who it was or what faith they believed in, we had to exercise *our* faith and belief. We prayed for Godly wisdom and for God's will to be done. At first I was a little leery. We had strange people coming around us from all over, and it was overwhelming. I remember sharing my feelings with my pastor, Samuel Smith, and he told me not to be afraid. Second Timothy 1:7 says God has not given us the spirit of fear but of power and of love, and of a sound mind. These words really helped me to be more confident and comfortable around the people we had to deal with.

This was the perfect opportunity to live out Matthew 5:16 "Let your light so shine before men, that they may see your good works and glorify your Father in Heaven." God pulled us out of darkness and into His marvelous light and made us new creatures. I believe my family was chosen by God to be a beacon light and offer hope to those who didn't know Christ or who did know Him but were out of fellowship with Him. If the people had pure motives, our spirits would connect, and if they came around for the wrong reasons the spirit wouldn't let them stay.

Every time a news person interviewed us, they were interested in knowing who raised Vincent because he was so humble, honorable, and respectful. God gave Vincent a humble heart. He was never arrogant and mouthy. He was born with a humble heart.

We had some very serious decisions to make about Vincent's college choice, and we truly put it in God's hands. He was the only one who knew the expected end for Vincent. It was prayer that led us to University of Texas. We visited the campus, listened to the presentations from the athletic department and about their academic program. I had to see if this was the school God wanted Vincent to go to. The first thing I asked the people we met with was if they believed in God. I was not going to leave my son in the hands of people who did not believe. A statement was made that they may not be a deacon or saint, but yes they did believe in God. That's all I needed to know about their salvation because I can pray to God about the rest.

I can honestly say our steps were ordered by the Lord, and the rest is His-story. Vincent was off to become a University of Texas Longhorn.

During Vincent's tenure at UT, prayer became an integral part of the football department. We would pray on the campus before and after the game. Vincent was praying on and off the field, and I was a praying sister in those stands with the parents and fans. We prayed for our children on and off the field, their success as football players, success in class and for protection from injury. I tell you, prayer brought us truly together as parents and families. We showed love and concern for one another, and God honored that and gave us favor and victory! We started out with just our family and friends praying along with Vincent Jr., but as the time passed the circle kept getting bigger and bigger. There were some people there for their own agenda, but we just kept being led by the Holy Spirit and being obedient to God. They are much stronger than ever by faith.

He had a very successful college football career. He was challenged, he exceeded the expectations of the naysayers, and he played for coaches Mack Brown and Greg Davis who believed in him and developed his game and molded him into a great leader. Vincent Jr., to this day, credits Mack Brown with making him a better man. And in turn, Vincent led them to victory in the 2005 national championship. I'll never forget those last twenty-six seconds. It was 4th and 5, and all I remember, is yelling, "Help him, Lord. Help him. Help him, Lord. Help him! Help him, Lord. Help him. All the way into the end zone."

It eventually became decision time for Vincent. Did he stay in college or enter the NFL draft? He came to me, and you know what I said? "That's between you and God, son." In my heart I know he wanted to enter the draft, but I also know he wanted to fulfill the promise he made to me and that's to be the first one in our immediate family to graduate from college. I was very supportive of Vincent's decision, and he is still determined to get his degree. In fact after his second season in the NFL, he attended the University of Texas during the off-season to pursue his degree. And he will finish.

In the Huddle

Reflecting upon his entrance into the NFL...

The Lord favored us because we tried to do things pleasing in His sight. There were people saying wrong things about Vincent and our family, but we had to look away and stay prayerful about that person or situation that was up against us. I just prayed, "No weapons formed against us shall prosper, in the name of Jesus." Sure it made me angry hearing things about my son, but we had to humble ourselves and pray. It was hurtful to turn on the TV or read people in the paper saying Vince couldn't throw, Vince couldn't comprehend, Vince couldn't stay in the pocket, and Vince couldn't read plays. I have to keep talking to Vincent and my family today to let them know if God be for us, who is going to be against us. As long as we stay on the right side we do not have to worry what man might do to us.

Sideline Chat

When God predestined you to fulfill His plan, no one can take away what God has given to you. If you are predestined, you are anointed by God to do His will. The Lord says touch not thy anointed, so don't worry about the haters and naysayers. God has the final say and you have the victory! God's Word says in Galatians 6:7, "Be not deceived, God is not mocked for whatsoever a man sow, that shall he also reap." What goes around comes around. All you should be concerned about is being obedient and be found doing things pleasing in the sight of God.

The Game Plan

The Bible says in 1 Thessalonians 5:17 to pray without ceasing. Keep praying for your loved ones. My knees look just like camel knees because I stay on them so much. All the prayers that were prayed by our great-grandparents, our grandparents, my mother and father, people who prayed for us are paying off. God gave me the responsibility of covering my family and everyone connected to us with prayer. I constantly prayed Psalm 91 over my friends and loved ones.

Matthew 25:21 says, "His lord said unto him, 'well done, thou good and faithful servant: thou hast been faithful over a few things, I will make thee ruler over many things: enter thou into the joy of thy Lord.'" In the end, this is what we all should want to hear, "Well done, my good and faithful servant." I came to this part of my life when the Holy Spirit began teaching me how to be a good steward over what God has given to me.

In the Huddle

God started setting me up when I was still out there doing my thang, as we use to call it. I was living it up. I had a really good job after I came off welfare. I was a home health aide at the time, seeing fifteen patients a day. The home health service was paying me sixteen dollars per patient a day. The money was good. I even received bonuses for quality work. I was able to give money to my mom to help with the bills and buy my children some of the things they wanted and needed. I still had a high alcohol and cocaine bill. So even though God provided me with a great job, it seemed like the more money I made the less money I had. Have you ever been there?

When the Holy Spirit prompts you to pray about the things He's placed in your heart, you'll find yourself praising, thanking, and asking God for forgiveness of your sins. With a pure heart fixed on pleasing God, it becomes easy to pray for your family, neighbors, church family, job, God's people, the leaders of our country, and the leaders of every nation, your enemies, unsaved folk, unchurched folk, rebellious believers, and the believers who are obedient servants. Practice the power of prayer. The life of someone you know and love depends on it! I know somebody prayed for me to come out of darkness. Hallelujah, I love His marvelous light.

Chapter 12

Winning Souls: Come from the **Weak Side**

> "Come unto me all ye that labour and are
> heavy laden, and I will give you rest."
> —Matthew 11:28

I lived on the weak side, and I know what it feels like. This destructive lifestyle was my choice. I've discovered as I've become closer and closer to God that I was trying to cover the pain of my past instead of allowing God to heal me from within. Jesus was wounded for our transgressions, and in Matthew 11:28, He instructs us to come unto Him all ye that labour and are heavy laden and I will give you rest. Laden means weighed down or burdened. The circumstances in our lives can truly make us feel this way, but I've come to share with you that God wants to bear this burden for us.

For the majority of my life, I carried my own burdens and it weighed me down, but life has new meaning for me since I cast all of my burdens upon God—and I mean *all*.

It's not always easy, but it is a necessity. When we try to do things on our own, God will allow us to. I can just see God sitting on the throne watching us cry, struggle, and fail at our experiences in life. I bet He's thinking if they would just have faith and believe in my Word I would give them rest. First Peter 5:7 tells us to —cast our burdens on Him because He cares for us.

As I've transitioned from the "weak side," I have committed myself to live a consecrated life. What is consecrated? I'm glad you've asked. It's a life devoted to God—Romans 12:1–2.

As elders now in the ministry, my mother and I have come into agreement to live holy unto the Lord so we may receive and do things God planned for us, as well as those who are connected to us. It is not an easy task. It's a tremendous responsibility and we have to stay prayed up and study God's Word daily. We are committed to being hearers and doers of the Word. I have made up in my mind to feast off the Word daily. Think of it this way: What would happen if you didn't feed your body food and water daily? You would shrivel up and die, right? That's exactly what happens to your soul when you do not read and know the Word of God—you shrivel up and die from the inside out. You have feelings of loneliness, sadness, depression, failure, defeat, and a myriad of insecurities, all because you don't know what God says about you.

Check out what God says about you in the Coach's Corner.

In the Huddle

As you've read, the devil had a plan to destroy my life since I was a teenager. I knew about God from my upbringing, but I had been hurt so much that I didn't have the faith in God to recognize the enemy's tactics. My self-esteem was low and I sought pleasure in stuff that I thought made me feel good. The devil tried to kill me through alcohol, drugs, cigarettes, adultery, and lying, among other things. I lied to myself, my family, and, shamefully, to God.

God made Adam and Eve and they disobeyed Him, which caused us to be destined for damnation. Thanks be to God that He did not give up on His own plan. He loved us so much that He gave us a way out through His Son, Jesus Christ, our Lord and our Savior. Who would have thought our unholy lifestyle before becoming a born-again believer would be our preparation for God's purpose. Like Adam and Eve, we've disobeyed God's statute and commands, and because of that we went through a series of shame, guilt, and poor self-image, lack of confidence, fear, anger, bitterness, and self pity. By not allowing God to order our steps, we became prideful, jealous, envious, covetous, hateful, and unforgiving. These spirits attached themselves to our lives, and they clouded our judgment and perception of God's plan.

I can't believe I listened to his lies. The enemy most definitely stole my marriage, my dreams, my accomplishments, and half of what God had given to me. He almost stole my children. Thanks be to God that He has the final say and all of my children are with me today. I want to bring glory to God by allowing my pain to become someone else's gain.

My faith has sustained me. I meditate on God's Word in Hebrews 11:6: "But without faith, it is impossible to please him: for him that cometh to God must believe that he is, and that he is a rewarder of them that diligently seek him."

Sideline Chat

To come from the weak side, you must purposely seek God who wants you to be a representation of Him. God is Love. He wants people to see you and experience love.

When dealing with people and situations, God wants us to handle things in a Godly manner. After all, we are all God's children—red, yellow, black, and white; we are all precious in His sight. As you've learned in Chapter 9, the Holy Spirit dwells within us and is always available to help us out. So when you are dealing with a situation you can't handle, remove self and selfish thoughts and ask the Holy Spirit to speak to you and give you the wisdom to do and say the right thing. Remember, the Holy Spirit is that still, small voice that instructs you to do the will of God. People are watching you, particularly your children. What are your actions teaching them? What do you *want* them to see and learn from you? Think about that!

When you have your daily time with God, I really encourage you to ask God for discernment of people and situations. Discernment is a spiritual insight to recognize clearly. It will really help to order your steps and know the difference between good and evil. You will begin to recognize who should and shouldn't be in your life. You will know if you are in the wrong place at the wrong time, and you will recognize if you are fulfilling God's game plan for your life. So remember, as you begin to walk in the goodness of God, ask Him for discernment and to order your steps.

God's Rookie

Now when you become a rookie on God's team, don't expect to be perfect. God is the only perfect one. You will continue to make mistakes, its human nature. He will send people to you who will mentor and support you. That person could be a pastor, spouse, relative, or even a new friend. You will know they are God-sent because they will provide wisdom, encouragement, and comfort to you. As scripture reveals to us in Titus 2:1-3, "But speak thou the things which become sound doctrine: That the aged men be sober, grave, temperate, sound in faith, in charity, in patience.The aged women likewise, that they be in behaviour as becometh holiness, not false accusers, not given to much wine, teachers of good things;" Here are a few tips on how to recognize your "teacher." Your teacher must have sound faith and be filled with love and patience. Your teacher must live in a way that honors God. They must not slander others or be heavy drinkers. Instead, they should teach others what is good. They must also be students of the Word and a living example of what they've learned. These are some of the same principles I live by as a mission sister when I go out into the community to care for others.

In the Huddle

I am a mission sister in my church. This has really helped me to be accountable to God and mindful of my actions. As a mission sister, I must be consistent in my behavior and actions and promote spiritual health in myself and others. I do this through prayer and studying God's Word. It is my responsibility to be available to listen, pray, witness, and evangelize to men and women of all ages.

Sideline Chat

Okay, young people, I know it's hard for you to listen to the ole folks because you think they are old and extinct, but I've learned so much in my life from the elders. They are wise, they listen, they are loving, and they have a great sense of humor. They truly have a way of lifting your spirit. It's amazing what you will learn about your history by just spending some time with an elder, and they can give you so much guidance for your future. How can you think you know so much when you haven't really gone through anything?

A disadvantage our young people have today is that parental styles have changed drastically. We need to go back to the basics. I remember sharing with a young mother that her nine-year-old daughter was too young to be wearing red fingernail polish because back in the day that represented a Jezebel spirit and fast girls wore red. She told me that was a myth and so old school, but what she failed to realize along with many parents today is that we give and expose our children to too much too soon. As a result, our children are out there with the temptations of the world, and they are too young and immature to handle them, then we have to pray, pray, pray to redeem them and bring them back into the fellowship of God to fulfill their purpose.

I am not saying we shouldn't adapt to the changing times, but I am saying old traditions could be healthy for our young people. Remember when dresses and shorts had to be a certain length, you couldn't wear pants and had to wear stockings to church? This was a form of worship to give reverence to God for the sacrifice He made for us. God wants us to let our bodies be a living and holy sacrifice that is acceptable in His sight.

As you become a member of God's team, don't copy the behavior and customs of this world, but let God transform you by changing the way you think and reveal to you His perfect and pleasing will for your life. Wherever God plants you for your spiritual growth (your church), understand God's order and be obedient. Understand the pastor is the under shepherd of the church. For example, His instruction comes from Jesus Christ through the Holy Spirit. If he says no pants, there should be no pants. When you do the opposite of what your pastor says, you are disobeying the Lord. Jesus is the Head of the church. Whoever your pastor tells you is the elder of your church, you must obey. When you are obedient, blessings come your way.

I live in Texas and sometimes I just want to be barefoot because it's hot and I want my feet to be comfortable, but I can't because the Holy Spirit will convict me about being obedient. It could also cause other young ladies to be disobedient. First thing somebody will say is "Sister So and So is not wearing stockings today." I know this sounds foolish but it's real. I do not want to cause anyone to stumble or stunt their spiritual growth. I must lead by example.

In the Huddle

Soul winning is my mission! If you are called to the responsibility in the kingdom of God, you must stay focused. This is not about us. This is about the Lord and the soul of man. Someone must live a life of Christ before those lost souls can be bound for glory. I am commissioned to do that.

John 15:16 says, "Ye have not chosen me, but I have chosen you, and ordained you that ye should go and bring forth fruit, and that your fruit should remain: that whatsoever ye shall ask of the Father in my name, he may give it to you." If the world hates you, ye know that it hated me before it hated you. If ye were of the world, the world would love his own: but because ye are not of the world, but I have chosen you out of the world, therefore the world hated you (John 15:18–19).

I believe I was chosen to go out and spread the gospel so people in this barren land would come to know God. I have learned from the best, my pastor, Pastor Smith! He is the father of street ministry. He has written a wonderful help manual—Taking it to the Streets—and he's an incredible teacher on witnessing in the streets. I have gone with him to the streets of Houston ministering to the lost and offering hope through Jesus Christ. It is a blessing to see people give their lives to God. That is our job as Christians who are committed to God's business. The way we live our very lives should have people wanting to know more about God. You should want to share the love and compassion that God restored to you. God loves the just and unjust. With witnessing comes reconciliation. We must be reconciled back to the Almighty—the Father—and with our family and neighbors.

Reconciliation is removing unforgiveness, hatred, envy, jealousy, and strife from our hearts. This is required to be an effective witness. We have to start at home first before we go out and witness where the undwell lives. Our lives must be lined up with Christ in order to enter in the devil's camp. When you go out to witness some things are done by fasting and praying.

If you make an impact on one person or a million people, you have helped change someone's life for eternity. Now don't you think God will be pleased with that? If God has delivered you from the world's system, you should really be compelled to help those who are where you use to be. That's one reason for this book because I want drug addicts, inattentive parents, and adulterers to know all you need is a touchdown from heaven, and you will be made whole.

Welcome to God's starting line-up!

Chapter 13

Now, It's Your Time: Cross the **Necessary Line**

"For I know the thoughts that I think toward you, saith the LORD,
thoughts of peace, and not of evil, to give you an expected end."
—Jeremiah 29:11

Get Ready for Your Promotion

There is hope. In the beginning, all God's children were included in His plan for sharing in His glory. Everything that was made by Him was good. We are destined for greatness. The purpose for our life was ordained before we were placed in our mother's womb. It's time to receive God's goodness.

Receive Your Spiritual Inheritance

Isaiah 43:18–19 says, "Remember ye not the former things, neither consider the things of old. Behold, I will do a new thing; now it shall spring forth; shall ye not know it? I will even make a way in the wilderness, and rivers in the desert."

God knows the plans He has for you. They are plans of progress and success, not defeat and failure. Although it's ten yards at a time, when you cross the necessary line you are getting closer to the end zone. I encourage you to give God the Father, your Lord and Savior, and the Holy Spirit your entire self—that is your mind, heart, soul, and body. It is God's desire that we prosper and be in good health, but when we put our ungodly choices first we interrupt the plan of God for our lives.

According to John 10:10, "The thief cometh not, but for to steal, and to kill, and to destroy: I am come that they might have life, and that they might have it more abundantly." This is in the Word of God. He wants us to have an abundant and fruitful life. However, we make a mistake when we desire material possessions more than we desire God who wants to be first and all these things will be added unto you (Matthew 6:33).

In our playbook, we must design a strategic game plan where we allow God to order our steps and follow the path of righteousness that will ultimately lead to our destiny. Begin to surround yourself with positive people and let your light shine among them. I remember about ten years ago, when I was trying to get my life back on track, one of my get-high buddies whom the Lord sent, told me I was going to be greatly blessed through my son, Vincent.

God's plan cannot happen and will not come to pass if we choose not to cooperate with God or to stray away from His will. I had to choose whom I was going to serve and accept His plan for my life, and I did it for my family. My acceptance of God's wills is what allowed His promise to come to pass for my family today.

Sideline Chat

As the scripture states Jeremiah 29:11, God has an expected end for each of us! Do you realize He created you for a purpose? Do you know what that purpose is? Do you wonder why you are no further in life than you are, or do you have it all and you are still unfulfilled?

Let's use me for example. We know, according to scripture, that God knew me before he placed me in my mother's womb. He had a purpose for my life. My destiny had been sitting right next to me all the time. God knew His plan for me, but I didn't notice it because I was so preoccupied with distractions of this world. You know the enemy comes to steal, kill, and destroy, and what does drugs, alcohol, adultery, lying, cheating, stealing, backbiting, and ungodliness have in common? They steal, kill, and destroy! When we let this stuff have control, we miss the opportunities and blessings God has for us.

Sometimes God's ways are just not what we had in mind, and we get all mixed up.

The beauty of it all is that God does not give up on us the way we give up on Him sometimes.

I want you to really meditate on Romans 12:2, "And be not conformed to this world: but be ye transformed by the renewing of your mind, that ye may prove what is that good, and acceptable, and perfect, will of God."

I challenge you to become intimately familiar with life's manual (the Bible), it was written for us! We have to know the Word to understand God's ways and His plan for our lives. Don't think of the Bible as an old history book. It has a right now Word for you and me. I promise if you begin reading it for wisdom, instruction, and guidance, I guarantee you will not fall asleep when you open it up. I know, I've had those days and people tell me all the time, "I try to read the Bible but me just get so sleepy."

If you fall asleep on the Word, you will sleep through the future God has planned for you. It is a future of peace and prosperity.

Many of us will walk past our destiny because we are too preoccupied with non-essential things—worthless things—that have in our present day taken center stage in our lives. Many of us will miss the opportunity of coming into our destiny and basking in the blessings God has ordained from the beginning of time for us because our focus is on the temporary and on the transient—things that will pass away. Many are the attractions of this world that steal our joy and turn our minds off the reality of life.

Philippians 4:6–9 says, "Be careful for nothing; but in every thing by prayer and supplication with thanksgiving let your requests be made known unto God. And the peace of God, which passeth all understanding, shall keep your hearts and minds through Christ Jesus. Finally, brethren, whatsoever things are true, whatsoever things are honest, whatsoever things are just, whatsoever things are pure, whatsoever things are lovely, whatsoever things are of good report; if there be any virtue, and if there be any praise, think on these things. Those things, which ye have both learned, and received, and heard, and seen in me, do: and the God of peace shall be with you." Tell God what you need, and thank Him for all He has done. If you do this, you will experience God's peace, which is far more wonderful than the human mind can understand. His peace will guard your hearts and minds as you live in Christ Jesus. And now, dear brothers and sisters let me say one more thing as I close this letter. Fix your thoughts on what is true and honorable and right. Think about things that are pure and lovely and admirable. Think about things that are excellent and worthy of praise. Keep putting into practices all you learned from me and heard from me and saw me doing, and the God of peace will be with you."

Thanks be to God that He is in charge over our lives. Because of the choices we made and the lack of knowledge of the Word of God, all our pain was for someone else's gain. Jeremiah 29:11 says, "For I know the thoughts that I think toward you, saith the LORD, thoughts of peace, and not of evil, to give you an expected end." The Lord sees not only what you are right now, but also He knows what you can become. He knows the plans He has for you. They are good plans and progress and success, not defeat and failure. I encourage you to give God the Father, your Lord and your Savior and the Holy Spirit your entire self to live in you to do our Father in Heaven's will on Earth. His plan for each of us is a plan that gives us great hope for our future. It is our destiny, but that plan is a possibility and not a positively—if you do not accept the plan God has for your life, you can miss what God actually has in store for you. If someone prophesied over us wonderful things in the name of the Lord, what they say to us may express the heart, the will, and the desire of God for us.

I had to choose whom I was going to serve and accept the plan for my life and my family life. It doesn't mean what was prophesied over my life was positively going to happen just as it was said. God's plan cannot happen and will not come to pass if we choose to refuse to cooperate with God or to stray away from His will. God does have a plan for our lives, but we have to participate in that plan for it to come true. God will not do anything in our lives without our desire to do what He asks us to do. We need to cooperate with God every single day of our lives in order for our potential to be developed. Every day we should want to learn something new. Every day we should want to grow. We are to discover something about our self. We are to be further along than we were the day before. We should be lifetime learners. We must discover our own God-given talents—what we are truly capable of—and then put ourselves to the task of developing those gifts, talents, and capabilities to their fullest extent.

The plan of God is a season of new beginning. Second Corinthians 5:17 tells us, "Therefore if any man be in Christ, he is a new creature: old things are passed away; behold, all things are become new." So let God line you up with His plan for your life in due season. All will be and your needs and your desires will be fulfilled in the new season.

Are you ready for the plan God has for *your* life?

Resources for Victory

Playbook for Salvation

An Invitation to Salvation

Understanding the Plan

Salvation is Free!

Why must I be saved (born again)?

John 3:3: "Jesus answered and said unto him, Verily, verily, I say unto thee, Except a man be born again, he cannot see the kingdom of God."

We have all sinned and fallen short of the glory of God (see Romans 3:23). The wages of sin is spiritual death, which is separation from God.

Romans 6:23: "For the wages of sin is death, but the free gift of God is eternal life through Christ Jesus our Lord."

Being spiritually dead means you are separated from God. If you die in this state, you will find yourself in eternal hell.

Revelations 20:15: "And whosoever was not found written in the book of life was cast into the lake of fire."

This is good news. His love is unconditional. Even before we accept Jesus, He loves us, but that doesn't mean we're saved until we accept His son and believe in the work He did for us on the cross.

Romans 5:8: "But God commendeth his love toward us, in that, while we were yet sinners, Christ died for us."

What does it mean to be saved?

When you are saved, you are as they say, born again! You are considered a new creation.
2 Corinthians 5:17: "Therefore if any man be in Christ, he is a new creature: old things are passed away; behold, all things are become new."

Once you accept Jesus Christ, you are a part of the family of God, and you will inherit eternal life.

1 John 3:1: "Behold, what manner of love the Father hath bestowed upon us, that we should be called the sons of God: therefore the world knoweth us not, because it knew him not."

God the Father loves you so much that He will forgive all of your sins. And there is no sin greater than another. Sin is sin, and He will forgive you.

Micah 7:19, "He will turn again, he will have compassion upon us; he will subdue our iniquities; and thou wilt cast all their sins into the depths of the sea."

Once your sins are forgiven, you are enclothed with the righteousness of God by faith in Christ Jesus

Romans 3:22: "Even the righteousness of God which is by faith of Jesus Christ unto all and upon all them that believe: for there is no difference."

Ephesians 2:6: "And hath raised us up together, and made us sit together in heavenly places in Christ Jesus."

Mark 16:15–18: "And he said unto them, Go ye into all the world, and preach the gospel to every creature. He that believeth and is baptized shall be saved; but he that believeth not shall be damned. And these signs shall follow them that believe; In my name shall they cast out devils; they shall speak with new tongues; They shall take up serpents; and if they drink any deadly thing, it shall not hurt them; they shall lay hands on the sick, and they shall recover."

Yes, the Word is true. Isn't it amazing that you will have inherited these powers to cast out demons and heal the sick? You will receive this authority by becoming a child of God.

We Are Not Saved by Our Works

It is important to know we are not saved by our works, but by faith in Christ Jesus and the work He did for us.

Titus 3:5: "Not by works of righteousness which we have done, but according to his mercy he saved us, by the washing of regeneration, and renewing of the Holy Ghost."

Our sins are completely paid for by the blood of Jesus.

Matthew 26:28: "For this is my blood of the new testament, which is shed for many for the remission of sins."

Do not try to earn your salvation or forgiveness of sins. You must realize it is faith in Christ that saves you, not your works. Good works should follow naturally as you grow in your relationship with God. After all, we will become more like Him as we grow spiritually.

Now that you know why you should be saved and what means to be saved is, here is how to assure you are saved...

What Must I do to be Saved?

Jesus paid the price for our sins when He went to Calvary; He shed His blood for the remission of our sins. Jesus truly stood in the gap for us when He went to the cross. In the Old Testament (before Jesus came), they would sacrifice animals to cover their sins, but now that Jesus paid the price, we no longer need to perform sacrifices. In the Old Testament, we could only cover our sins with the blood of animals, but the blood of Jesus actually removes our sins. It erases it from our account altogether.

Hebrews 10:4: "For it is not possible for the blood of bulls and goats to take away sins."

John 1:29: "The next day John seeth Jesus coming unto him, and saith, Behold the Lamb of God, which taketh away the sin of the world."

Hebrews 10:17: Then he adds, "And their sins and iniquities will I remember no more."

The blood of Christ was shed for our sins, and through faith in the work that was done for us, we can be freely justified—that is, made right with God:

Romans 3:24–26: "Being justified freely by his grace through the redemption that is in Christ Jesus: Whom God hath set forth to be a propitiation through faith in his blood, to declare his righteousness for the remission of sins that are past, through the forbearance of God; To declare, I say, at this time his righteousness: that he might be just, and the justifier of him which believeth in Jesus."

Steps to Your Salvation

1. Your first step is to believe in your heart that Jesus Christ is the son of God, who came to earth (living in a human body), was crucified, and died for your sins, and then rose again on the third day.

John 3:16–17: "For God so loved the world, that he gave his only begotten Son, that whosoever believeth in him should not perish, but have everlasting life. For God sent not his Son into the world to condemn the world; but that the world through him might be saved."

Acts 16:30–31: "And brought them out, and said, Sirs, what must I do to be saved? And they said, Believe on the Lord Jesus Christ, and thou shalt be saved, and thy house."

2. Second, confess with your mouth the Lord Jesus Christ (affirm your belief verbally). This is usually what we refer to as the prayer of salvation.

Romans 10:9-10 "That if thou shalt confess with thy mouth the Lord Jesus, and shalt believe in thine heart that God hath raised him from the dead, thou shalt be saved. For with the heart man believeth unto righteousness; and with the mouth confession is made unto salvation."

Prayer of Salvation

Believe in your heart and say this prayer and you shall be saved.

"Lord Jesus, I believe you are the son of God and that you came to Earth and died for my sins and rose again on the third day. I confess I am a sinner and in need of your salvation. I come to you now and ask that you will come into my life, be my Lord and savior, and forgive me of my sins. In Jesus' name. Amen!"

So Now that I'm Saved, What Do I Do Next?

After being born again, it is important to cultivate your new relationship with Christ Jesus. You do this by spending time in God's Word daily. As you meditate on God's Word, it will begin to change the way you think. Your mind will be renewed and transformed, and strongholds (old thinking patterns) begin to come down. This is vital to your spiritual freedom and wholeness.

Romans 12:2: "And be not conformed to this world: but be ye transformed by the renewing of your mind, that ye may prove what is that good, and acceptable, and perfect, will of God. "

Ephesians 5:25–27: "Husbands, love your wives, even as Christ also loved the church, and gave himself for it; That he might sanctify and cleanse it with the washing of water by the word, That he might present it to himself a glorious church, not having spot, or wrinkle, or any such thing; but that it should be holy and without blemish.."

Ephesians 3:17–19: "That Christ may dwell in your hearts by faith; that ye, being rooted and grounded in love, May be able to comprehend with all saints what is the breadth, and length, and depth, and height; And to know the love of Christ, which passeth knowledge, that ye might be filled with all the fulness of God."

SELF-DELIVERANCE

PROVERBS 6:5 "...DELIVER THYSELF..."

If you want to get rid of your temper, lustful thoughts, actions, or any other demons, you can do self-deliverance. There are times when there is no one around to help us. It is at this time that we must be able to do self-deliverance. Our body is the temple of the Holy Spirit and we must be able to command our bodies to the attention of the Lord and His Word and take back the land that the enemy has taken.

Before being able to get help, you must be a real Christian.

To become a Christian, Romans 10:9 says, "That if thou shalt confess with thy mouth the Lord Jesus, and shalt believe in thine heart that God hath raised him from the dead, thou shalt be saved." You must believe Jesus is the Son of God, that He died for your sins, and that you are sorry for and repent of your sins.

Sincerely say this prayer: "Father, in Jesus' name I ask you to forgive me of all my sins. I repent, Lord. Come into my life. Fill me with the Holy Spirit. With your help, I will stop sinning. In Jesus' name. Amen."

For any deliverance, the only requirements are:

1. You have repented and ask Jesus to save you. In other words, you must be a true worshipper (John 4-23).
2. You have forgiven everyone who has ever hurt you.
3. You want deliverance from the demons (evil things/thoughts/ spirits) in your life.

You must forgive everyone who has ever hurt you in any way. This is legal ground for the demons to be in you, and they do not have to come out. I don't care who calls them out.

Say, "Father, in Jesus' name, I forgive my father, mother, brothers, sisters, relatives, (name anyone else), and anyone else who has ever hurt me."

Unforgiveness has been known to cause you not to be blessed.

If you meet these requirements, then say the following prayer: "Father, in Jesus' name I cover myself and this place with the blood of Jesus. I bind up all my demons and the demons in this place. I ask for giant warrior angels to surround this place to protect me."

Pray the above prayer every time you start a new deliverance session.

Make a list of all the things in your life you want to get rid of (don't add your spouse to this list).

Now, for each demon say, "I command temper (or whatever) to come out of me now. Come out of my conscious, subconscious, and unconscious mind, all parts of my body, will, emotions, and personality, in Jesus' name.: You can name the demons one by one or a few at a time. Almost anything you can imagine is a name of a demon. The power and authority are in the words *In Jesus' name*, or any rendition of His name. If you haven't tried it, how can you say it doesn't work?

Don't ask Jesus to do it. He told you to do it, using His name.

After calling each demon, take a deep breath and blow out though your mouth. Demons come out through tears, air passages like your mouth (coughing, yawning, and mucus), nose running, passing gas, through the skin, or no visible signs at all. You don't have to feel or see anything to be set free. No one knows all the answers, but I know when you blow out it helps dislodge demons. When finished with each deliverance session, pray, "Father, in the name of Jesus, I ask you to fill me fuller with the Holy Spirit. Fill all the nooks and crannies where all the demons have left."

Remember that Jesus said the demons consider you their house. When the demons leave some of their rooms, you must fill them with something (Holy Spirit, praying, worship, reading your Bible). Luke 11:24–26 says, "When the unclean spirit is gone out of a man, he walketh through dry places, seeking rest; and finding none, he saith, I will return unto my house whence I came out. And when he cometh, he findeth it swept and garnished. Then goeth he, and taketh to him seven other spirits more wicked than himself; and they enter in, and dwell there: and the last state of that man is worse than the first."

These scriptures make it clear why it is necessary to do deliverance daily. Spiritual warfare is necessary all during the day. This just supplements the deliverance process. Spiritual warfare is designed to be offensive and not defensive.

You know you are free of a particular demon when you no longer do the demon's job (i.e., lie, curse, pornography, steal, fear, etc.).

Jesus did deliverance daily, and so should you. Luke 13:32 says, "And he said unto them, Go ye, and tell that fox, Behold, I cast out devils, and I do cures to day and to morrow, and the third day I shall be perfected." Even a satanist can be set free. In the name of Jesus, you can break any blood oath you made with the devil. I read that most homosexuals wished that they could stop being homosexual. Deliverance can change you, too. You really can stop doing things you don't want to do except for paying taxes. Jesus loves you that much.

Recap for Deliverance

1. You must be saved before you can cast demons out of yourself and others. Say this out loud:

"Father, in Jesus' name, I ask you to forgive me of all my sins. I repent, Lord. Come into my life. Fill me with the Holy Spirit. With your help, I will stop sinning (John 5:14). Amen."

2. You must forgive others. Say this out loud: "Father, in Jesus' name I forgive my mother, father, brothers, sisters, aunts and uncles, any other relatives, and anyone else who has ever hurt me." (Name any other people who come to mind.)

3. Start kicking demons out in the name of Jesus! Say this out loud: "Father, in Jesus' name I cover myself with the blood of Jesus, all my family members, everyone seeking deliverance, and this property that I am now in. I bind up all the demons in me and around me, and in everyone seeking deliverance, in the name of Jesus. I ask for giant warrior angels to protect us, in the name of Jesus."

"I thank you, Lord, for giving me all power and all authority over all demons, in the name of Jesus. I take that authority now, and I command all these demons to start coming out now, in the name of Jesus. You come out of the conscious, subconscious, and unconscious minds, all parts of the body, will, emotions, and personality, in the name of Jesus. I terminate your assignment and break all legal holds, in the name of Jesus. I go back to Adam and Eve, on both sides of the bloodline, and I chop you off at the roots, in the name of Jesus." Now just start calling out the demons one by one or a few at a time. We recommend doing the basic list of demons first, and then make your own list of things in your life you want out and start calling them out, in the name of Jesus.

Examples would be:

Temper; come out in the name of Jesus!

Lust; come out in the name of Jesus!

Religiosity, come out in the name of Jesus!

False gifts come out in the name of Jesus!

Preparations and Precautions

This is a basic step-by-step outline of how to go about self-deliverance. This is not a complete set of instructions that will work for everybody, and if you need to be freed from heavier bondages, you may be better off consulting with an actual deliverance minister if you are able to locate one. These instructions will give you a good idea of how to drive demons out of yourself. It is recommended that you read up further on this subject before attempting to run yourself through deliverance.

The limits of self-deliverance: Self-deliverance is very helpful in many situations where a deliverance minister isn't available to minister to you, and you can be set free from much bondage simply by running yourself through a self-deliverance. However, it can be limited if compared to a regular deliverance session.

Precaution: If you have come out of heavy or active involvement in the occult or Satanism, you would be better off seeing an experience deliverance minister to minister deliverance to you, because the demons encountered in those situations are usually much stronger and are best off handled by somebody else.

If you begin to feel like you are losing control as a demon manifests, then stop and seek help from an experienced deliverance minister.

Pre-deliverance prayer: As with any deliverance, it is good to pray that the Holy Spirit will show you what the roots to the problem are, and what needs to be done. Pray for His continual guidance and strength during the deliverance session. It is often helpful to ask God to send angels to assist in the deliverance. They can play a powerful role in helping you flush the demons out.

Warning to nonbelievers: Deliverance is for believers (Matthew 15:22–28), and is not fit for unbelievers (those who are outside the covenant). If you aren't a Christian, I wouldn't even attempt deliverance because it's like stirring up a hornet's nest. First, accept Jesus, and then seek deliverance. This way, you can prevent the demons from returning with several more even worse evil spirits as Jesus warns in Matthew 12:43–45. If you aren't a believer, I wouldn't even try to cast a demon out of anybody. As we can see in Acts 19:13–16, it's not wise to cast demons out if you aren't a child of God. They did not have authority in Jesus because they were unbelievers and seven men got thrown out of the house naked and beaten by the demon. As you can see, it's not wise or safe to attempt deliverance without Jesus in your life!

Prayer and fasting: Prayer and fasting always help prepare you for deliverance. Jesus said that some kinds of demons will only come forth through prayer and fasting, which build your faith to the higher levels required to cast some demons out.

1. Knowing what is rightfully yours

If you don't believe what is rightfully yours, it's going to be hard to claim it. Some of the things you need to have down pat are knowing your sins are forgiven, knowing you are a child of God, and knowing you have authority over the demons.

You need to understand who you are in Christ. This sounds simple, and is often overlooked, but is vital to your deliverance. If you don't really believe you are who you are, then you won't have the faith to stand on who you are and claim what is rightfully yours. If you don't really know you're a child of the King, you won't feel like a prince, and you won't act like a prince. And how are you supposed to defeat the enemy when you don't think like a child of God should? If you struggle with this, you need to tear down one or more strongholds.

You need to know your sins are forgiven. If you have guilt hanging over your head, then it will greatly hinder your ability to stand up to the enemy with a clear conscience and stand up for what is rightfully yours. Guilt is a door opener and keeper, and the enemy often uses it as a base to launch all sorts of attacks against God's children. You need to understand the nature of God and how freely Jesus wants to forgive you of all your sins. Luke 7:47 is one of my favorite verses the Lord showed me one time when I needed to learn this principal. It tells of how freely Jesus forgave a very sinful woman from all her sins without hesitation! Another good story on the forgiveness of our sins when we turn to God in repentance is found in Luke 15. If you struggle with obsessive guilt even after repenting of your sins and turning from them, then you need to tear down one or more strongholds.

You need to have a correct perception of God and your relationship with Him. If you see God incorrectly, you're going to be an easy target for the enemy. If you see God as a cruel taskmaster, you'll act like He's a cruel taskmaster and you will put up walls that will block you from feeling God's love. Furthermore, the enemy moves in with the power of suggestion (little things he whispers into your thoughts) and can terrorize the daylights out of you. If you think of anybody (husband, wife, boss, etc.) as a cruel, mean taskmaster, it puts up a wall and you see that person differently, don't you? Even though you could be completely wrong in your perception of them, to you, they are a taskmaster in your eyes, and therefore you shut them out of your heart. This is what we do to God when we see Him as a cruel and distant taskmaster. We cut ourselves off from experiencing and feeling His love. If you don't feel God loves you, then you need to back up and take a moment to review how you are perceiving Him. Many people struggle with this, and it is a stronghold that needs to be torn down.

You need to know the authority you have been given by God over the enemy. You, as a believer, have been given authority over all powers of the enemy, and you have been given the authority to bind and loose in the spiritual realm. You exercise your authority through a spoken word in faith. Just as Jesus cast demons out with His word, you can also cast demons out with your word, which is backed by the authority Jesus gave us as believers. You have the authority whether you feel like it or not, as long as you are a believer. It is important to know your authority is accessed through faith, and therefore the more you believe in your authority, the more of it you will be able to exercise. Mark 16:17 tells us that them who believe will be casting out demons in His name! There's a great teaching just on your spiritual authority that you may want to check out.

As I've mentioned, there's often the need to tear down strongholds in our lives. There's an excellent teaching just on strongholds that you may want to go through before attempting a self-deliverance if you sense there's any strongholds that need to be torn down.

2. Find the open doors and break off any legal grounds.

I believe this is one of the most important parts of the deliverance process. It is important to find out what opened the door to the enemy so we can close it and void their legal right to bother us. There are a number of ways he can gain access: through sins, ancestral sins caused by ancestral curses, unforgiving heart that blocks God's forgiveness toward us, dabbling in the occult, demonic vows, fear, etc. Rather than including a more complete list in this outline, there is a whole separate teaching just on legal rights and how to go about breaking them up.

3. Identify the areas of bondage in your life.

It's important to know what areas of your life are in bondage and a good idea of exactly what you are seeking to be set free from. Make a list of the things you want to be freed from. Know exactly what you want to be set free from, and then try to identify the open door that allowed the enemy to move into that area of your life. When did it start? If you had it your entire life and your parents or grandparents struggled with the same or similar problem, then it was likely generational. Often you can locate what opened up the bondage, if you look back around the time in your life when it started. It's always a good idea to become familiar with the various ways the enemy can gain access into our lives. A good understanding of legal rights and strongholds is always helpful. There is a deliverance questionnaire posted on this site to help knowledgeable ministers identify areas of bondage in a person's life. This can be helpful to even an unexperienced person who has a general understanding of legal rights and strongholds.

It's always a good idea to make some lists pertaining to your bondage. A list of legal rights is good and can help you keep track as you are going through the list and breaking up those legal grounds. A list of the areas of bondage in your life is always a good idea. A list of strongholds is also a good idea to keep track of. If you need further deliverance from another minister or need more deliverance in the future (not all bondages are broken in one session—it often takes multiple sessions to completely set a person free—it can be very helpful to keep track of what is going on. If you seek further ministering from an experienced minister, presenting those lists to him or her can give them a good quick look into your situation and can save them time trying to uncover the areas of bondage in your life.

4. Cast out the demons.

Take authority over the demon spirits within you by issuing a command such as, "In the name of Jesus, I now take authority over every evil spirit present within me, and I command each and every one to submit to the authority invested in me by Jesus Christ!"

If you can address the demons by name (lust, anger, suicide, hate, fear, etc.), you will often find them submitting to your authority easier because it makes it harder on them to write you off as if you weren't talking to them. If somebody yelled "hey you!" in a crowd, you probably wouldn't pay any attention to them, but if they yelled out your name, you would be a lot quicker to respond. The same is true with demons. If you address them by name, they are a lot easier to get their attention. Notice how many times Jesus addressed the demons, such as deaf and dumb spirits, by name.

Not every deliverance session requires you to refer to the demons by name, but it sure helps when you are able to get ahold of their names, either through remembering your previous involvement with evil spirits (if you accepted a spirit guide by the name of Daemon, then obviously Daemon needs to go), another way to get the name is by the symptoms they are causing. For example, extreme guilt is often caused by a spirit by the name of guilt, and other ways to get their names are by a word of knowledge from the Holy Spirit, or from the demons themselves (ask them for their name and listen for their response).

If I have a demon's name handy, I often like to use it. If not, I just proceed without it.

Using your authority in Jesus, command the evil spirits (by name if possible) to come out of you in Jesus' name! Don't be alarmed if you find yourself throwing up all of a sudden, or coughing uncontrollably, screaming, etc. It's a good sign. It usually means they are on their way out!

If you want to minimize manifestations, you can forbid them to manifest in Jesus' name. I usually like them to manifest because it exposes them even more, and somehow weakens their power and cocky attitude when they are hauled out in the open where you can recognize them.

5. Encountering groupings of demons.

Demons often work in teams, and if you identify the strongman, it will help you in figuring out their game plan and give you a better idea of how to go about casting out certain demons first and unraveling their scheme. This is important because this strongman is usually the big guy you are going after. Once you cast him out, the lesser demons usually follow suit much easier. However, sometimes it's better to cast out the lesser demons, and then deal with their leader after they are all gone and he can no longer play games or hide behind them.

Since demons communicate with other demons both within and outside of you, I like to forbid and shut down their communication between each other. I like to issue a command like this, "I now shut down and forbid all lines of communication between the evil spirits within me, between themselves, and with those outside of me in Jesus' name!"

6. Binding and loosing.

Binding is a temporary spiritual handcuffing. If you get worn out and need to continue deliverance the next day, you could simply bind the remaining demons and continue the deliverance later. Binding is also helpful when ministering to somebody else. You can bind and forbid the demons to interfere with the person as you work with them to tear down strongholds, break up legal grounds, etc.

Loosing is referring to removing a captive from bondage. Jesus loosed the woman from a spirit of infirmity in Luke 13:12. You might say something like, "I loose myself from the spirit of fear in the name of Jesus! Spirit of fear, I command you to come out in the name of Jesus!"

7. Checking to see if you are free.

You should feel a noticeable relief when the demon(s) have left. However, they may just be hiding and trying to trick you into calling it a success, only to rear up their heads later on. Pray and ask the Holy Spirit to reveal to you if there are any demons remaining that need to be cast out or whether the deliverance was successful. The long-term effect after a deliverance is usually your best indicator, but when there have been symptoms of the demon (such as fear, anger, suicidal urges, etc.), then I would expect those to be gone when the deliverance has been successful.

Don't forget to consider that in many cases, deliverance is a process and not just one session. If strongholds need to be torn down that the demons are hanging onto, they can usually take time as you tear them down. When the spirits leave you though, you should feel the difference and be able to freely walk in your newfound freedom.

8. Post-deliverance instructions.

I don't walk in constant fear of demons returning, but I also advise not to dabble in the things that opened you up to demons in the first place either. Keep your relationship with God cultivated, and don't let the enemy tempt you to let him back in.

If you are unsuccessful, seek further knowledge on the ministry of deliverance and consider seeking the help of an experienced deliverance minister. Don't forget to consider that in many cases, deliverance is a process and not just one session. If strongholds need to be torn down that the demons are hanging onto, they can usually take time as you tear them down. If you try your best and are getting nowhere, then I would seek help from an experienced minister.

Spiritual Roadblocks

Not willing or ready. As elementary as this sound, much deliverance is unsuccessful because the person was not ready or willing to be truly delivered. They were merely looking for a quick fix for their problem and were not willing to take the necessary steps to receive and maintain their deliverance.

Unforgiveness. Bitterness is a very popular source of spiritual defilement (Hebrews 12:14). If you don't forgive others, God will not forgive you (Matthew 6:15). Unforgiveness puts us in the hands of tormenters (Matthew 18:23–35), which are demonic spirits.

Strongholds. Strongholds are incorrect thinking patterns in our minds that we see things through. Many people see themselves as failures, so they feel like failures. Others see God as a cruel and dictating taskmaster, which causes them to feel distant and unloved by their Heavenly Father. If you have a hard time feeling God's love, you can cast out all the demons in the world, but if you don't see God as a loving God who loves you, it's going to be very difficult to feel and receive His love.

Unconfessed sins. If we confess and repent of our sins, God is faithful and just to forgive us (1 John 1:9). But if we choose rather to keep our sins hidden and to ourselves, we cannot expect God's forgiveness. There is also power in confessing our faults to one another. As James 5:16 tells us, "Confess your faults one to another, and pray one for another, that ye may be healed. The effectual fervent prayer of a righteous man availeth much."

Soul ties. Having a soul tie with somebody means your soul is joined with theirs (1 Corinthians 6:16). Being joined to another person with an unclean soul tie can allow the transference of spirits and bondage between the persons. It is vital to break off all bad soul ties from unhealthy past relationships so the enemy cannot use them against us.

Cursed objects. The Bible gives us a clear pattern of destroying false gods, idols, and so-called cursed objects. God warns us that bringing a cursed object into our home can bring a curse upon us as well (Deuteronomy 7:26).

Lack of faith. Not understanding or believing God's will or the truth about your situation can keep you in bondage as well. If you don't realize the authority and freedom you have in Christ, it can be very hard to walk in it and eat of its fruit. Knowledge of the truth is indeed an important tool in our spiritual toolkit.

Unrenounced vows. Vows and oaths bind the soul (Numbers 30:2). The way to break free from any ungodly vows is to repent and renounce it verbally in Jesus' name.

Unbroken curses. Both ancestral curses and curses encountered in one's own life must be broken. I believe ancestral sin curses are automatically broken so long as we have accepted Christ, and do not take part in our ancestor's wickedness, but other types of curses must be broken before complete deliverance can be obtained and kept.

Residing spirits. Demons often need to be cast out of a person before they are able to fully overcome much persistent bondage. Demons are often found behind many issues such as fear, depression, physical infirmities (arthritis, cancer, deafness, etc.), or mental illnesses and need to be driven out as Jesus and the early church went about doing.

SEEKING GOD

"Sow to yourselves in righteousness, reap in mercy; break
up your fallow ground: for it is time to seek the LORD,
till he come and rain righteousness upon you."
—Hosea 10:12

What does it mean to seek God?
A. The psalmist well-described man's search for God when he cried,
   "deep calleth unto deep…" (Psalm 42)
B. It is the spirit of man longing for fellowship with God.
   Psalms 63:1, 6–8; 84:2–3
   Song of Songs 3:1–4
   Isaiah 26:9
   John 4:23–24
   Romans 1:9
   Philippians 3:3

I. The very purpose of man's existence is to seek God.
   Acts 17:26–28
   A. Failure to seek after God results in spiritual death.
      Isaiah 5:13
      Hosea 4:6
   B. But an impartation of His life through us can be obtained by
      seeking Him with all our hearts.
      Deuteronomy 30:6, 19–20
      Psalm 69:32
      Proverbs 8:34–35; 14:27; 19:23
      Amos 5:4, 6, 8
      John 14:6

III. He promises those who diligently seek him shall find Him.
    Deuteronomy 4:29–31 (Jeremiah 29:11–14)
    1 Chronicles 28:9
    Psalm 9:10
    Proverbs 8:17
    Matthew 7:7 (Luke 11:9–10)
    John 6:37
    James 4:8
  A. We do not seek Him in vain.
    Isaiah 45:19
    Malachi 3:13–14
  B. He promises certain blessings and rewards to those who diligently seek His face.
    Psalm 107:9
    Lamentations 3:25
    Hebrews 11:6
    1. Joy.
      Psalm 70:4; 105:3
    2. Peace and rest.
      2 Chronicles 14:7; 15:12–15
    3. Revelation.
      Jeremiah 33:3
    4. Understanding in the ways of God.
      Proverbs 28:5
    5. Strength.
      1 Chronicles 16:11
      Psalm 105:4
      Isaiah 40:31; 41:1
    6. Prosperity and provision.
      2 Chronicles 26:5
      Psalm 34:9–10
      Matthew 6:33
    7. Security.
      Psalm 27:4–5

IV. God requires an immediate response on our part to the beckoning of the Spirit.

Psalm 27:8

A. The Lord, like a timid deer, is withdrawn.
Song of Songs 2:9

B. We must not delay when He calls (Song of Songs 5:2–6), but seek the Lord while He may be found (Isaiah 55:6).

C. Continued delay to the call of the Spirit may result in the hardening of our hearts (Hebrews 3:7–8, 15), and cause that the consciousness of His presence be withheld from us.
2 Chronicles 32:31
Song of Songs 5:2–6, especially verse 6
Hosea 5:15.

V. God seeks those who will seek Him.
2 Chronicles 16:9
Psalm 14:2; 53:2
John 4:23

A. Continually.
1 Chronicles 16:11

B. Wholeheartedly.
2 Chronicles 15:12
Psalm 119:2, 10
Jeremiah 29:13
Hebrews 10:22

C. Diligently.
Psalm 63:1
Proverbs 8:17
Isaiah 26:9

D. Above all else.
Psalms 27:4; 73:25-26
Matthew 6:33

✦ Only God can touch our hearts and give us the desire to seek and to know Him, and to want His will and plans and ways above our own:

"And I will give them an heart to know me, that I am the LORD: and they shall be my people, and I will be their God: for they shall return unto me with their whole heart." —**Jeremiah 24:7**

"O LORD God of Abraham, Isaac, and of Israel, our fathers, keep this for ever in the imagination of the thoughts of the heart of thy people, and prepare their heart unto thee: And give unto Solomon my son a perfect heart, to keep thy commandments, thy testimonies, and thy statutes, and to do all these things, and to build the palace, for the which I have made provision." —I **Chronicles 29:18–19**

"For it is God which worketh in you both to will and to do of his good pleasure."—**Philippians 2:13**

+ Intimacy with God and the fullest possible fellowship and partnership with Him comes as you desire and seek to know Him and His plans and will and His ways. Prayer and spending time with God are all about desire and passion for God. It is not a religious discipline in your Christian walk.

"Now therefore, I pray thee, if I have found grace in thy sight, shew me now thy way, that I may know thee, that I may find grace in thy sight: and consider that this nation is thy people. And he said, I beseech thee, shew me thy glory.." —**Exodus 33:13,18**

"One thing have I desired of the LORD, that will I seek after; that I may dwell in the house of the LORD all the days of my life, to behold the beauty of the LORD, and to enquire in his temple." —**Psalm 27:4**

"As the hart panteth after the water brooks, so panteth my soul after thee, O God. My soul thirsteth for God, for the living God: when shall I come and appear before God?" —**Psalm 42:1–2**

"O God, thou art my God; early will I seek thee: my soul thirsteth for thee, my flesh longeth for thee in a dry and thirsty land, where no water is; To see thy power and thy glory, so as I have seen thee in the sanctuary. Because thy lovingkindness is better than life, my lips shall praise thee." —**Psalm 63:1–3**

"How amiable are thy tabernacles, O LORD of hosts! My soul longeth, yea, even fainteth for the courts of the LORD: my heart and my flesh crieth out for the living God.." —**Psalm 84:1–2**

"Now set your heart and your soul to seek the LORD your God; arise therefore, and build ye the sanctuary of the LORD God, to bring the ark of the covenant of the LORD, and the holy vessels of God, into the house that is to be built to the name of the LORD." —**I Chronicles 22:19**

"And thou, Solomon my son, know thou the God of thy father, and serve him with a perfect heart and with a willing mind: for the LORD searcheth all hearts, and understandeth all the imaginations of the thoughts: if thou seek him, he will be found of thee; but if thou forsake him, he will cast thee off for ever." —**I Chronicles 28:9**

"For I know the thoughts that I think toward you, saith the LORD, thoughts of peace, and not of evil, to give you an expected end. Then shall ye call upon me, and ye shall go and pray unto me, and I will hearken unto you. And ye shall seek me, and find me, when ye shall search for me with all your heart." —**Jeremiah 29:11–13**

"Yea doubtless, and I count all things but loss for the excellency of the knowledge of Christ Jesus my Lord: for whom I have suffered the loss of all things, and do count them but dung, that I may win Christ, And be found in him, not having mine own righteousness, which is of the law, but that which is through the faith of Christ, the righteousness which is of God by faith: That I may know him, and the power of his resurrection, and the fellowship of his sufferings, being made conformable unto his death; If by any means I might attain unto the resurrection of the dead." —**Philippians 3:8–11**

Also: **Hosea 10:12, James 4:8, Deuteronomy 4:29, 2 Chronicles 15:2, Matthew 6:33, Proverbs 21:21**

"God looked down from heaven upon the children of men, to see if there were any that did understand, that did seek God." —**Psalm 53:2**

Obedience—Christians are to obey the word of God

"Teaching them to observe all things whatsoever I have

commanded you: and, lo, I am with you always, even unto
the end of the world. Amen." —**Matthew 28:20**

"And Samuel said, Hath the LORD as great delight in
burnt offerings and sacrifices, as in obeying the voice of
the LORD? Behold, to obey is better than sacrifice, and
to hearken than the fat of rams." —**1 Samuel 15:22**

**Jesus said blessed are those that hear Word of God and think about
it.**

"But he said, 'Yea rather, blessed are they that hear
the Word of God, and keep it." — **Luke 11:28**

Scripture teaches it is right for children to obey their parents.

"Children, obey your parents in the Lord:
for this is right." **Ephesians 6:1**

**Peter said sometimes it is better to obey God over the laws of the
land.**

Obedience is greater than sacrifice. Through obedience we become a
treasure to God.

"Now therefore, if ye will obey my voice indeed, and keep
my covenant, then ye shall be peculiar treasure unto me
above all people: for all the earth is mine." **Exodus 19:5**

Obedience brings blessings.

"And it shall come to pass, if thou shalt hearken diligently
unto the voice of the LORD thy God, to observe and
to do all his commandements which I caommand thee
this day, that the LORD thy God will set thee on high
above all nations of the earth." **Dueteronomy 28:1**

Obedience can bring prosperity and pleasure.

"If they obey and serve Him, they shall spend their days in prosperity, and their years in pleasures." **Job 36:11**

Solomon was promised a long life if he obeyed God.

"And if thou wilt walk in my ways, to keep my statutes and my commandements, as thy father David did walk, then I will lengthen thy days." **1 Kings 3:14**

The wrath of God comes to those who disobey.

"Let no man deceive you with vain words: for because of these things cometh the wrath of God upon the children of disobedience. **Ephesians 5:6**

It is not a good practice to associate with the disobedience to win them.

"And if any man obey not our word by this epistle, note that man, and have no company with him, that he may be ashamed." **2 Thessalonians 3:14**

We will obey sin if we allow it to remain in our life.

"Let not sin therefore reign in your mortal body, that ye should obey it in the lusts thereof." **Romans 6:12**

Submitting to God is the first step in resisting Satan.

"Submit yourselves therefore to God. Resist the devil, and he will flee from you." **James 4:7**

Obedience should come from the heart.

"Servants, obey in all things your masters according to the flesh; not with eye service, as men pleasers; but in singleness of heart, fearing God." **Colossians 3:22**

By faith and being warned of God of things not known, Noah obeyed God and built an ark.

> "By faith Noah, being warned of God of things not seen as yet, moved with fear, prepared an ark to the saving of his house; by which he condemned the world, and becae heir of the righteousness which is by faith." **Hebrews 11:7**

By faith Abraham obeyed God and went into an unknown country.

> "By faith Abraham, when he was called to go out into a place which he should after receive for an inheritance, obeyed; and he went out, not knowing whither he went." **Hebrews 11:8**

People were amazed than unclean spirits had to obey Jesus.

> "And they were all amazed, insomuch that they questioned among themselves, saying, What thing is this? What new doctrine is this? For with authority commandeth He even unclean spirits, and they do obey Him." **Mark 1:27**

Even the winds and sea obey the voice of God.

> "But the men marveled, saying, "What manner of man is this, that even the winds and the sea obey Him!" **Matthew 8:27**

Sharing a little more with you..........

Raising Boys to Become Men

"Train up a child in the way he should go and when he
is old, he will not depart from it." — Proverb 22:6

Five Key Points in Raising Boys to Become Men

+ Moms should give lots of love while their boys are young, and they
should spend quality time with them. Proverbs 17:17 says, "A friend
loves at all times."

  Moms must give much love while their sons are young and spend
much quality time with them, making sure they are observant and
watchful for their sons' individual gifts. They also must make sure
they have all they need—clothing, food, playing time, rest, and
homework. They must encourage them when they succeed and
encourage them when they do not make it and tell them to keep on
trying until they succeed. They must tell them the dos and the don'ts
in family down time, TV, music, sports, and church. Teach them to
say their blessing over their food before eating and tell them why you
bless your food. Have family gatherings so they can learn to love and
share with others. Spend time with their friends until they finish
school. Take them with you on outings. Teach him to be gentlemen
by letting them be responsible for manly chores around the house
and when you are taking care of responsibilities.

+ Moms must be firm and discipline with much love. Proverbs 13:24
says, "He that spareth his rod hateth his son: but he that loveth him
chasteneth him betimes."

  If your children are without a father in the home, moms have to
be firm and show they mean business. Our greatest responsibility

God gives us is to nurture and guide them. The lack of discipline puts your parenting love in question. Those knuckleheads will try to buck you and then you have to spare the rod. It's going to take some whipping. If you do what God says He will guide you on How to spare the rod. The lack of discipline will show a lack of character development. Discipline shows love. Discipline is making sure your son is taught wrong from right. We mothers have to remember our efforts cannot make your children wise. We can only encourage them to seek God's wisdom above all else.

♦ Moms living with respect show the son to have respect for women. Proverbs 11:16 says, "A gracious woman retaineth honour: and strong men retain riches." First Timothy 3:4 says, "One that ruleth well his own house, having his children in subjection with all gravity."

A kind-hearted woman gains respect if you have respect for yourself and your son will see that. Then he will have respect for you and how you relate to men when they come around. Make sure healthy male figures are around, but stay away from sleepovers and profanity. We must work, fear God, and be responsible when we are doing outings, paying for meals, movies, and games. Adult activities belong away from the house and not around our sons.

You may find out our sons love drinking alcohol as well, but we should not do it in front of them. Sow only the seeds in your children lives that you want to reap through them down the road. What you sow you will reap. I'm a witness.

♦ If you live a Godly life, it sets the paths for sons to live longer. Proverbs 11:19 says, "As righteousness tendeth to life: so he that pursueth evil pursueth it to his own death."

A true righteous man attains life. We parents have to teach and live the life of Christ before our children as our elders live Godly lives before us. Our elders pave the way for us to live Godly lives and with abundance. This means being a teacher of good things. You have to teach your son to be responsible as if you were teaching that girl to be a responsible woman. They too need to know what chores are. They need to know how to live right, along with the proper diet and exercise and plenty of rest. Allow them to do things according to their time of growing up. They need to know they have to take responsibility for their actions. Teach them to work hard and to take care of their own.

+ Teach your sons to pray through your prayer life and to be thankful to God and get instructions from the Lord. Luke 18:1 says, "And he spake a parable unto them to this end, that men ought always to pray, and not to faint." Colossians 3:15 says, "And let the peace of God rule in your hearts, to the which also ye are called in one body; and be ye thankful." Proverbs 3:5–6 says, "Trust in the LORD with all thine heart; and lean not unto thine own understanding. In all thy ways acknowledge him, and he shall direct thy paths."

+ In order to do all things in Christ who strengthens you to do, you must pray faithfully and turn your children or your son over to the Lord and trusts Him to direct your path and your son's path. God knows the plan for your life and your son's life, so you want the Lord to line your life up with His will so He can line up your son's life because if you live the life your son will follow, meaning teach him, according to Matthew 6:33 to seek God first. Bringing them in the circle and locking hands in prayer for you and your family's needs will teach them to go to God in prayer and it will teach them to fear God.

Reaching Out and Touching the People in the Community

We who are the people of God are called out of darkness into the marvelous light through God's Son, our Lord and Savior Jesus Christ, which is the plan of God to reach out and touch the people in our community. Before we can help somebody we have to accept the salvation and deliverance plan in order to have the love of God for His people to be saved and delivered. In order to be effective in helping the needs of our fellow man, our neighbors, our sisters and brothers in Christ, the unsaved and the unchurched, we have to have a desire to help. We have to help all people, not just the ones we know. We must have a compassion for all people of God.

What my family found out was our foundation was built on the teachings of my grandmother Eliza Owens and my grandfather Smith Owens. They lived the life of Christ. They lived the life of prayer at the table, thanking the Lord and asking Him to bless our food at breakfast, lunch, and dinner. They prayed in the morning, at noon, and before we went to bed at night. The foundation was laid of helping our neighbors, friends and relatives. They helped the sick and were there for the bereaved families. While my grandparents made preparations to feed our family, they would transport anyone who needed to go the grocery store over in Palestine. Whatever their neighbor or family needed, no matter when, where, or what my grandparents did what they could. They believed in supporting all churches, so that meant we stayed in church all day every day because some meeting at the church was taking place, and they would be there faithfully. They were just being about the business of God. These things were passed down to my mom, Bonnie Pearl Owens, and my aunt Jessie Mae Owens. These ways of God were sowed in our family in order for us to have a compassion for people. It has to start in the home. Teaching the love of God starts at home first.

The Lord said in 2 Corinthians 9:7–8, "You must each decide in your heart how much to give, and don't give reluctantly or in response to pressure, for God loves that person who gives cheerfully. And God will generously provide all you need. Then you will always have everything you need and plenty left over to share with others." In order to please God in your servitude you have to be dedicated to God (2 Corinthians 8:5); provide information (2 Corinthians 8:4); show definite purpose and goals (2 Corinthians 8:4); be enthusiastic (2 Corinthians 8:7, 8, 11); reveal honestly and integrity (2 Corinthians 8:21); be accountable (2 Corinthians 9:3); let people give willingly (2 Corinthians 9:7); be generous yourselfers (2 Corinthians 8:7), have someone to keep it moving (2 Corinthians 8:18–22); be persistent, trusting God to provide (2 Corinthians 8:21).

To be successful in helping our community we have to bring structure, kindness, information about our health, our schools, our children, our families, our leaders, and our churches. We have to fundraise, which gives us an opportunity to give of ourselves. In order to do this we cannot be embarrassed about fund-raising efforts. It should be planned and conducted responsibly. This is to help the needs of our people. Sometimes applying for 501(c) 3 non-profit organizations will help to meet a need. Seek out resources.

Whatever gift God gave to you and you have done well with it, it's time to give back to God's people. God gave everyone a gift—some more than others. You must use what you are good at and you must glorify God with it. If there is anything you desire, ask God to have the Holy Spirit to set you up and prepare you for what you desire to do. You have to ask our Heavenly Father what is your purpose and to line you up with your purpose in the name of Jesus. When you pray to Him, wait on Him to set you in position. In the meantime your mission will be rendering aid to the sick, visitation in the prisons, help some mother with their child, talk and pray with your neighbors and for your neighbors, transport somebody to church, to the doctor, to the store or for a outing. Help out the schools, be a team mom if you have an athlete in the home, make sure the children are educated.

We have much work to do. Our Lord is on His way back as we speak. He says in His word that He comes when you least expect it and we who are born-again believers, children of God, must be found doing works of God with love in our hearts. This is so our labor will not be in vain. You will hear from Him, "Servant, well done." It's never too late to do the things of God. Pray always; study the Word of God; go to Bible study, Sunday school, and prayer and teachers meeting; and keep your family, neighbors, leaders, and pastor lifted up in prayer. Live what the Word says and be an example and a teacher of good things. Then you will see the results of God's people coming together in unity, increasing and living in abundance. Step out on faith, believe, receive, and share what God gave someone to share with you. Be a blessing. Thank you.

Turning Difficult Times into Excellent Times
2 Timothy 3:1–7

We born-again believers, we children of God, are living in the last days of difficult times. Second Timothy 3:1–7 where Paul writes to Timothy about the life of Christians, telling what God had promised us through faith in Jesus Christ. He tells us through God's Word that the last days will be very difficult times. He says people will love only themselves and their money and they will be boastful and proud, scoffing at God or will mock Him, disobedient to their parents, and ungrateful. They will consider nothing sacred and have no self-control. They will be cruel and hate what is good. They will betray their friends, be reckless, be puffed up with pride, and love pleasure rather than God. They will act religious, but they will reject the power that could make them Godly. Paul tells us to stay away from people like that. He also warns us they will work their way into people's homes and win the confidence of vulnerable women who are burdened with the guilt of sin and controlled by various desires.

I want to stop right here for a few minutes. This seems so real to me because I remember when I was one of those vulnerable women. After my husband left me I was so devastated. I thought the man I married loved me and he was going to take care of me and I thought he was a family man. I thought he was going to care for the children and me. Well, the dream did not work that way. There was another plan. My husband left the children and me for a life of whatever he wanted to do. During the years of the children growing up, through all my hurt and pain I was determined to take care of my children, no matter what. I said it's all about what I wanted to do. You know where those lead me, to a life of destruction. Anytime you do what self wants and it is not of God, you run right dead smack into Satan himself through all the love you tried to find in all the wrong places. I ended up taking on other people's relationships, meaning they were having relationships with drugs, alcohol, and adultery—everything that had to do with the night life. My sisters, we have to be careful more now than ever. We women, young or old, cannot allow ourselves any longer to be victims of other people mistakes. We must find ourselves in God. We must accept the plan God has for us through Jesus Christ. We have to take the stand for God and His righteousness and take our rightful place as life givers. We are the ones who have to pray for our children and men so they will take their rightful places in God's kingdom. We have to keep a covering over everyone around us by pleading the blood of Jesus over them. Pray faithfully. Live the life of Christ before mankind, so that we know all things work together for the ones who love God and are called according to His purpose. If we do not, we women will forever follow new teachings and will never be able to understand the truth. Opposing the truth is opposing the Gospel of Jesus Christ. This will cause us to have depraved minds and a counterfeit faith. We need to be watchful and stay prayed up.

We who are our Father's children can be victims in such a time as these. God gives us a way to be or stand while dangerous times are here.

In Ecclesiastes 8:5 we learn the ones who obey God will not be punished. Those who are wise will find a time and a way to do what is right for there is a time and a way for everything, even when a person is in trouble. Galatians 6:9 tells us the advantage becomes excellent times when we put all our trust in God. When we do not get tired of doing what is good, at just the right time we will reap a harvest of blessing if we don't give up.

Paul tells us in the beginning of time in 2 Timothy 1:9, God saved us and He called us to live a holy life. He did this, not because we deserved it, but because that was His plan from before the beginning of time—to show us His grace through Christ Jesus. Through the Good News of Jesus Christ, God loves us, He chose us, and He sent Christ to die for us so we can have eternal life through faith in Him. He broke the power of death with His resurrection. We do not deserve to be saved, but God offers us salvation anyway. We can have peace in the midst of the storm if we believe Him and have accepted His offer or plan. I know for a fact we can live a good life in the last days, but only through living that holy life unto God be faithful to Him, while He is being faithful unto you.

Everything that is going on has already been prophesied in the book of Revelation. We are the children of God, and He will withhold no good thing from you if you love Him and obey His Word. All that is not living the righteousness of God are the ones who will be cut down like grass. The Lord is on His way back as we speak, and we must not waste anymore time about being life givers. We must go out and tell somebody about the goodness of God and Jesus Christ so that they lives can be changed. Trust God. All will be well, no matter what happens, if you believe.

You Are Called for Such a Time as This

"For if thou altogether holdest thy peace at this time, then shall there
enlargement and deliverance arise to the Jews from another place;
but thou and thy father's house shall be destroyed: and who knoweth
whether thou art come to the kingdom for such a time as this?"
—Esther 4:14

Queen Esther was asked to do something very difficult in order to help
bring deliverance to her people. Most likely, she did not feel like being
in the challenging place where God had put her. She probably did not
want the responsibility, nor did she want to risk the personal harm she
knows could come to her. Esther was a young maiden with her whole life
ahead of her. Leaving her dreams behind, she was being asked to follow
instructions from the Lord that seemed very dangerous. She was to go
before the king to expose a wicked plot that had been launched against
the Jews. No one was allowed to go before the king unless he or she was
invited, not even the queen. Esther knew that unless God gave her favor,
she would be killed. I would say that Esther put everything on the line
in order to obey God's will.

Mordecai, who was speaking to Esther on God's behalf, told her she
must not keep silent. If she did, people would perish. He reminded her
that perhaps she had been called to the kingdom for the very task that
lay before her.

If Jesus Christ had not called me through a friend who once was
in darkness with me, God turned his life around and then used him to
preach the Gospel. God moved on Him and told him to go back and
witness to us in the neighborhood and tell what thus said the Lord and
about the goodness of God.

While I was in my mess, God used my brother Reverend Bill Brown to come and speak a word to my bosom and to tell me He was going to greatly bless me through my son, Vincent Jr. Well, I thought, *what does that mean?* If his hands had not been on me, I could have died with my riotous living being an alcoholic, drug addict, adulterer, liar, or smoking two packs of cigarettes a day. I could have died of cirrhosis of the liver, emphysema, HIV, or with busted blood vessels in the heart, clogged arteries, and a frozen heart where blood could not get to the heart or a heart attack. If I had not bowed down on my knees and humbled myself to Jesus Christ, my Savior and Lord, and confessed and repented all of my sins and asked Him for forgiveness, I would have been greatly blessed without deliverance. Some people were born blessed with everything and did not work for it—it was just passed down—but they do not have a piece of Heaven right here on Earth and that's God Holy Spirit. They are not free to live in the abundance of God to serve and to do His will. Being greatly blessed is the abundance of God.

What the Holy Spirit also gave to me to share with you was from the beginning of time, in Adam and Eve's day of disobedience, everything had to change because we serve a Holy God, and when God instructs us in something He means it. Nothing He says can go back void. Down through the years because of disobedience of God's people, we have gone through some stuff by choice. Because of our choices, self, Satan, and sin caused us to go through struggling within. We just wanted to do what we thought was right. After we suffered the consequences some learned from their mistakes and some still do things their way and not God's way. But think about God, how He provided for us and how He brought us through with His love, Jesus Christ, and with His grace and mercy. He saw to it that we were not destroyed or killed. We had a lot stolen from us by the devil. For me, it was my self-esteem, my marriage, great jobs, money, homes, my dreams and my goals.

But look at God! He has raised us up for such a time as this. He said the wicked would be brought down and the riches would be turned over to the righteous. The riches are put in the hands of the righteous, and we are being raised up. What are we going to do? The Father says when He raises us up not to forget about Him, meaning do not stop praying and communicating with Him, helping someone else to help themselves, not hinder them by letting them think it's you and not God. Continue to be about the Father's business. The riches in the hands of the righteous is to help God's people, to lead them to Christ while meeting a need, to bring the tithes into the store house so His people will be fed, so all that you are going through and have been through is being used for such a time as this. God is no respecter of person. What He did for me He can do for you. All things work together for those who love God and are called according to His purpose.

You, too, may be alive today in order to fulfill the purposes of God in your generation. The timing and place of your birth are not accident. God purposely and specifically places us all in certain time frames and places. Many people spend their entire lives never knowing their own destiny rather than following the leading of the Holy Spirit. Following God receives sacrifices and a willingness to be uncomfortable. Esther reached a point of being willing to die if she needed to in order to obey God who places us in a position for a purpose, so we can trust Him and seek His guidance, then seize the moment and act. When it is within our reach to save others, we must do so.

In a life-threatening situation, don't withdraw, behave selfishly, wallow in despair, or wait for God to fix everything. Instead, ask God for his direction, and act! God may have placed you where you are for just such a time as this. Be confident He will do His part. You don't know ahead of time how he will accomplish His will. Trust God and prepare to be surprised by the ways he demonstrates His trustworthiness.

IF You Successfully followed the instructions
that God gave me, then I say to you

TOUCH DOWN!!!!!!!!!!

I will see you in Glory. HALLELUJAH TO THE
LAMB OF GOD Thanks love yawl

MS. Lisa

About the Author

Felicia Young, from Houston, Texas is the mother of popular former Madison High School, University of Texas – Austin standout and currently the Tennessee Titans quarterback, Vincent Young. Throughout the struggles of her life, including, alcohol, drugs and domestic violence, GOD has changed her life and has commissioned her over 11 years ago and has commissioned her to minister to the nations about the gospel. Ms. Young is desirous of helping others through her faith-based ministry and music. The ministry mission statement is "To meet the Social, Charitable, and Educational Needs of the Nations". The ministry has a vision to empower women of all ages and ethnic groups. Her clients will be women who have faced and are facing difficult times, "especially those experiencing domestic violence, re-entering for the workforce from incarceration, as well as former drug addicts." Her vision is to provide a safe haven for those women at a live-in housing. The Felicia Young Ministries has four immediate visions: Community Gospelfest, Soul Winning Conferences, Prison Ministry, and Women Transitional Homes. With the vision of the ministry, GOD has commissioned her to write her first book called "Touchdown from Heaven, which elaborates more on the struggles of her life and how she overcame her situations with GOD.